FOR TEACHERS, PARENTS & KIDS:

Strategies That Promote Self-Esteem, Achievement and Behavioral Self-Control

James Battle Ph.D.

James Battle and Associates
#406 Edwards Building
10053 - 111 Street
Edmonton, Alberta
T5K 2H8

International Standard Book Number: 0-9695950-6-9

Canadian Cataloguing in Publication Data

Battle, James
    For Teachers, Parents and Kids

Includes index.
ISBN 0-9695950-6-9

1. Self-esteem in children. 2. Achievement motivation in
children 3. Self-control in children I. James Battle and
Associates. II. Title
BF723.S3B37 1994   155.4'1825   C94-910839-1

My Favorite Teacher

My favorite teacher provided me care,
    unconditional positive regard and respect
Which made me realize that I was worthy
    and could stand strong and erect.

My favorite teacher provided me encouragement
    and opportunities to be heard and seen
Which set the base for positive self-esteem.

My favorite teacher was firm, gentle and kind
A dedicated instructor and true friend of mine.

My favorite teacher provided me knowledge and wisdom
    and challenged me so I could see
The goodness in you and me.

My favorite teacher made learning clear to me
So that I could see the value of knowledge for you and me.

Even when my favorite teacher disagreed
    with my point-of-view
I knew that this teacher's caring for and prizing me grew.

My favorite teacher taught me the difference
    between right and wrong
How to serve others and make them feel that they belong.

My favorite teacher taught me
    how to study, plan, work and play
How to prepare myself for graduation day.

My favorite teacher was my model, my mentor, my friend
Who supported me from beginning to end.

                James Battle

Table of Contents

PART I:
Background Information

PART II:
Promotion and Enhancement Strategies

PART III:
Recommended Reading and
Self-Esteem Resource Materials

PART IV:
Glossary of Terms, References
and Indexes

Acknowledgements

THE WRITER GRATEFULLY ACKNOWLEDGES the support of the many individuals who contributed to the development and publication of this book. First, I thank the parents, teachers and children who provided me the opportunities to interact with them over the years while serving as a researcher, clinician, school and counselling psychologist. Second, I thank the schools and agencies who permitted me to test the strategies described in the book. Third, I thank my daughter Christina and secretary Maria Smith for the many hours they put in typing the book. Fourth, I thank my wife Dorothy and mother-in-law Edith Cary for reading the book and making editorial suggestions. Fifth, I thank Martin Barry and Edie Brewster for the excellent work they did in producing the book. Sixth, I thank my family Dorothy, Christina and Jamie for their unconditional love and the support they provided me during the term of this project and over the years.

Finally, I dedicate this book to all caregivers who support children and their families and strive to promote their physical, mental and spiritual well being.

Preface

IN THIS PRACTICAL, CONCISE BOOK we describe time-tested strategies that can be used by teachers, parents and other care providers to promote the self-esteem, academic achievement and behavioral self-control of children and students.

In writing this book, concerted efforts were made to produce a text which incorporates strategies that can easily be implemented systematically by teachers, parents and other care providers while interacting with children and students. The book is written in a style with vocabulary that can be readily understood by teachers, parents, other professionals and lay audiences as well.

THE BOOK IS ORGANIZED IN FOUR PARTS.

PART I provides background information and an overview of the crucial variables of self-esteem, achievement and behavior. In this part, we emphasize the importance of self-esteem and propose that it (self-esteem) is a crucial variable that exerts a strong effect on the lives of individuals comprising all cultural and socio-economic groups. In this part, we also tell readers what self-esteem is and list characteristics of the construct. In addition, in this part we provide overviews of the issues of self-esteem, academic achievement and behavior and propose that self-esteem, academic achievement and behavior are clearly interrelated.

PART II. In this part, we ask the important questions "Can teachers enhance self-esteem and achievement?" and "Can parents enhance self-esteem and achievement?"

We propose that both teachers and parents can enhance the self-esteem and academic achievement levels of kids and describe strategies that both caregivers can easily implement systematically. Because of this position, we describe strategies that teachers, parents and other care providers can use to promote the self-esteem and academic achievement of kids.

In addition, in this part, interactive strategies that have proven to be effective in enhancing self-esteem and academic achievement and behavioral self-control are described. Also, in this part, readers are shown how to develop and implement self-assessment procedures and problem resolution strategies.

Finally, we show teachers, parents and other care providers who instruct kids how to implement a preventative model which promotes behavioral self-control.

PART III provides an annotated list of recommended readings and self-esteem resource materials.

PART IV provides a glossary of terms, a list of references and subject and author indexes to the book.

Introduction

SELF-ESTEEM, ACADEMIC ACHIEVEMENT AND BEHAVIOR are important issues that have attracted considerable attention from individuals occupying a wide array of roles in our contemporary society.

Self-esteem is a prominent and persistent need which exerts a major influence on the lives of humans at all levels. For instance, self-esteem affects one's accomplishments, achievement patterns, ability to adjust to environmental demands and interpersonal relationships with others *(Battle, 1987, 1990, 1993, 1994)*. Nathaniel Branden *(1969)* in his manuscript entitled *The Psychology of Self-Esteem* states "I regard self-esteem to be the single most powerful force in our existence... the way we feel about ourselves affects virtually every aspect of our existence: work, love, sex, interpersonal relationships of every kind." Support for Branden's position is provided by Bowman *(1966)* when he stated:

> It is generally assumed that the way a person thinks of himself determines the general intent and direction of a person's behavior. In other words, persons who think of themselves negatively will behave in self-defeating ways, even though they may choose a variety of behavior patterns in the process *(pp. 76 - 77)*.

Gurney *(1988)* in his manuscript entitled *Self-Esteem In Children With Special Educational Needs* proposed that self-esteem permeates the child's whole life and potentially influences every single learning situation and action which he undertakes.

Self-esteem is associated with mental health and psychological well being, self-defeating patterns such as under-achievement, conduct disorders, oppositional defiant disorders, attention deficit hyperactivity disorders and psycho-pathological conditions such as depression, anxiety disorders, suicidal ideations and completions.

Self-esteem is also associated with achievement. Those students who achieve at or above grade level generally experience higher levels of self-esteem than their counterparts who achieve at lower levels. For instance, I *(Battle, 1979)* studied 134 boys and girls enrolled in grades one to seven and found that the students who were experiencing learning problems earned lower self-esteem scores. These data indicate that the children who were experiencing learning problems earned self-esteem scores that were significantly lower than those who were apparently making satisfactory academic progress.

A significant proportion of students who experience learning problems and low levels of self-esteem drop out of school *(O'Connor, 1985; Depauw, 1987; Rumberger, 1987; Wehlage and Rutter, 1986)*. These students with low self-esteem who drop out of school also experience more intense symptoms of depression *(Battle, 1986, 1988, 1990)* and more frequent suicide attempts. In addition, these students tend to experience more intense symptoms of anxiety and more difficulties with legal authorities which often result in periods of incarceration, pregnancy at an earlier age and more frequent incidences of legal and illegal substance abuse *(Battle, 1988, 1992, 1993)*.

Data derived from research findings also indicate that self-esteem is associated with behavioral problems such as

Attention Deficit Hyperactivity Disorders. Support for this position is provided by findings of a research study conducted by Battle and Shea *(1989)* which indicate that students enrolled in grades one through twelve with ADHD earned lower self-esteem scores than those who were not experiencing this condition. The findings reported by Battle and Shea *(1989)* support the position which purport that behavioral problems such as Attention Deficit Hyperactivity Disorders generally exert a negative effect on the self-esteem of experiencing children.

At this point in our development there is an important crucial need to develop and implement methodologies and strategies that are effective in promoting the self-esteem, academic achievement and behavioral self-control of children and students.

This book represents my efforts to share with readers strategies that I have found to be effective in assisting students and clients while working as an educator, school psychologist and therapist.

PART I

Background Information

CHAPTER 1
Self-Esteem, Achievement And Behavior

Self-esteem, achievement and behavior are crucial variables that effect the lives of all residents. Because of this, there is an important need to develop and implement strategies that promote self-esteem, achievement and age-appropriate "desirable" behavior.

Self-Esteem

Although some individuals propose that *"The Self-Esteem Movement Is A Longstanding One That Has Been Promoted For Generations"*, this position is a commonly held misconception. Actually, the emphasis on self-esteem is a recent development. For instance, in 1982 I published a book entitled *"Enhancing Self-Esteem and Achievement"* in which I proposed that there was a crucial need for educators to attend to students' self-esteem needs in order to assist them in developing their potential more effectively. I made this argument because the percentage of under-achievers among our school-age population was high and because traditional methodologies that attended only to the cognitive aspects of school-age students simply were not working. The emphasis on self-esteem emerged because of the lack of the success that educators were experiencing in their attempts to assist students in developing their potential more effectively.

3

Although the construct of self-esteem has received serious attention by researchers and clinicians only recently, it is an age-old problem with roots in the most popular book of all ages, *The Holy Bible*. For instance, the words of Christ, recorded in John 13:34 reads "A new commandment I give you, that you love one another." The construct of self-esteem is also embedded in the views of classical writers such as Goethe who stated "the greatest evil that can befall man is that he should come to think evil of himself." However, in recent years the phenomena of self has attracted considerable attention from researchers. For instance, Gordon and Gergen *(1968)* conducted an extensive review of literature and found 2,500 publications that address the issue of self.

Self-esteem is a factor which encompasses all aspects of human behavior. For instance, Branden *(1983)* states that no significant aspect of our thinking, motivations, feelings or behavior is unaffected by our self-evaluations.

THE IMPORTANCE OF SELF-ESTEEM

In recent years the construct of self-esteem has attracted the attention of individuals occupying a wide variety of positions and gained prominence in the fields of education and mental health.

The importance of this force is summarized by Assemblyman John Vasconcellos in *Resolution Number 65* in which he states "The epidemics of violence, drug abuse, teen pregnancy, child abuse, chronic welfare dependency and educational failure threaten to engulf our society, and it appears that self-esteem may be our best hope for a preventative vaccine to develop an immunity to these and other destructive behaviors" *(p. 97:60)*.

Additional support for the important role that self-esteem plays in our contemporary society is provided by Pete Wilson, Governor of the State of California, in the following proclamation

A PROCLAMATION
by the
Governor of the State of California

WHEREAS, an understanding of one's multidimensional talents, innate worth, intuitive power, and ability to achieve and contribute are essential elements of self-esteem; and

WHEREAS, with self-esteem comes confidence, motivation, responsibility and many other characteristics that enable individuals to do their best and reach their full potential; and

WHEREAS, healthy self-esteem among citizens results in positive social and economic benefits that are crucial to fostering a more cooperative, productive, caring and forward-reaching society — one focused on seizing opportunities, rather than reacting to crises encouraging citizens to work proactively together to protect our future and that of our children; and

WHEREAS, the understanding of self-esteem provides an engine driving quality and improvement — quality in our work, creative endeavors, relationships, intellectual pursuits, daily experiences and overall lives; and

WHEREAS, a person's inner security derived from healthy self-esteem is also at the heart of a vital democracy, enabling individuals and organizations to function optimally in a multiculturally diverse environment; and

WHEREAS, for the past three years, Self-Esteem Month has been celebrated in California to focus on the need to promote self-esteem statewide: and

WHEREAS, this year's observance will emphasize the connection between self-esteem and quality, and its applications for society, business, and government;

NOW, THEREFORE, I, PETE WILSON, Governor of the State of California, do hereby proclaim February 1993 as Self-Esteem Month in California to emphasize self-esteem as a significant factor in the health, happiness, and productivity of all Californians.

IN WITNESS WHEREOF I have hereunto set my hand and caused the Great Seal of the State of California to be affixed this 12th day of January 1993.

Pete Wilson

Governor of California

ATTEST: *March Fong Eu*
Secretary of State

In the following letter to John Vasconcellos Assembly-man, State of California, who provided impetus to the recent self-esteem movement, Bill Clinton expresses his interest in the construct of self-esteem.

STATE OF ARKANSAS
OFFICE OF THE GOVERNOR
State Capital
Little Rock 72201

July 2, 1991

The Honorable John Vasconcellos
State Assemblyman
P.O.Box 301
Santa Clara, CA 95052

Dear John:

I am still interested in the Self-Esteem issue. We had some progress incorporating it in Arkansas during our most recent legislative session and hope to do more. The DLC has recently been inundated with suggestions for incorporation to its policy platforms, but this is one I am suggesting; hopefully we can get something accomplished soon.

I will keep in touch.

Sincerely,

Bill Clinton

For Teachers, Parents and Kids:

Dorothy Briggs, a major contributor in the field, summarizes her views regarding the importance of self-esteem in the following fashion:

> A person's judgement of self influences the kinds of friends he chooses, how he gets along with others, the kind of person he marries, and how productive he will be. It affects his creativity, integrity, stability, and even whether he will be a leader or a follower. His feelings of self-worth form the core of his personality and determine the use he makes of his aptitudes and abilities. His attitude toward himself has a direct bearing on how he lives all parts of his life. In fact, self-esteem is the mainspring that slates each of us for success or failure as a human being.

I consider self-esteem to be a fundamental need and one of the most important variables affecting the lives of individuals at all stages of development. Self-esteem affects one's:

- accomplishments
- interactions with others
- achievement patterns
- levels of mental health
- state of well being
  (Battle, 1992, p. 22; 1993, p. 19).

SELF-ESTEEM: WHAT IS IT?

Recently writers have offered an abundance of information addressing the issue of self-esteem. However, their views regarding the construct of self-esteem tend to differ. For instance, Youngs *(1991),* proposed six ingredients of self-esteem: physical safety, emotional security, identity, affiliation, competence and mission; Borba *(1989)* proposed five building blocks of self-esteem: security, selfhood, affiliation, mission and competence; whereas Reasoner *(1986)* proposed five components of self-esteem: a sense of security, a sense of identity or a self-concept, a sense of belonging, a sense of purpose and a sense of personal competence. This lack of consensus regarding what self-esteem is and what is needed to enhance it creates confusion for both beginner and mature readers.

Battle *(1981, 1982, 1988, 1992, 1993, 1994)* defined self-esteem in the following fashion:

> "... Self-esteem refers to the perception the individual possesses of his/her own worth. An individual's perception of self develops gradually and becomes more differentiated as he/she matures and interacts with significant others. Perception of self-worth, once established, tends to be fairly stable and resistant to change."

To understand what self-esteem is, one must visit briefly with Freud's psychoanalytic theory. Freud proposed that the personality is comprised of three components or sub-systems, the id, ego and superego. The id is the original part of the personality that contains all instincts. The id is the most powerful aspect of personality that contains the psychic energy or libido which is the major driving force of the personality. The id is the reservoir of man's innate primitive, biological drives (e.g. sex, thirst, hunger, aggression). Freud proposed that the id operates in accordance with the pleasure principle. Thus, its major concern is to reduce tension and obtain immediate gratification. The id at all times attempts to avoid pain and increase pleasurable experiences.

For Teachers, Parents and Kids:

The id, according to psychoanalytic theorists, represents the primitive purely selfish portion of personality which is not concerned with reality or moral factors. The id utilizes what Freud calls primary-process thinking, a primitive or infantile level of thinking which makes no allowances for reality.

The ego, unlike the id, is capable of reasoning and utilizing intellectual resources to provide gratification for the id and deal with the demands of reality simultaneously. The ego is the rational segment of the personality which utilizes properties such as judgement, perception, recognition and memory to permit the id to obtain tension reduction in an acceptable fashion. Thus the ego utilizes what Freud calls secondary process thought (intellectual resources), in its efforts to permit id gratification. The ego is the mediator and controller of the personality which operates in terms of the reality principle, that is, it operates in accordance with environmental demands. Therefore it has the delicate and often conflicting task of delaying id gratification and permitting its expression only when environmental demands are receptive to such expression.

The ego is an efficient system, but it is limited because it does not consider moral aspects of functioning. Therefore, Freud developed a third component of personality which he called the superego. The superego is comprised of the conscience and ego ideal. The conscience represents our views regarding what we consider to be right or wrong, whereas the ego ideal represents what we feel we "ought" to do or be. Hence self-esteem emerges from the ego ideal which is a consequence of early interactions between parents or parent surrogates and the child. Thus, self-esteem is a subjective construct which is strongly tied to personality, namely the ego-ideal portion of Freud's superego.

CHARACTERISTICS OF SELF-ESTEEM: HIGH AND LOW

Findings reported by a number of investigators (*e.g. Cohen, 1957; Coopersmith, 1967; Branden, 1983; Battle, 1987, 1990, 1992*), indicate that there are distinguishing features that characterize individuals who possess high or low self-esteem. For instance, A.R. Cohen *(1957)* reports that individuals who possess high self-esteem, (as compared to those with low self-esteem), are characterized by tendencies to protect themselves from negative self-evaluation. Cohen *(1957)* also claims that individuals with high self-esteem (as compared to those with low self-esteem) are more effective in their ability to evaluate successes and failures objectively attributing accurate degrees to either.

HIGH SELF-ESTEEM
Individuals with high self-esteem:

1. tend to be more effective in meeting environmental demands.
2. tend to be more autonomous, and usually manifest greater confidence that they will succeed than individuals with low self-esteem.
3. tend to successfully defend themselves against threats and demeaning attempts by others.

The individual with high self-esteem generally considers himself to be capable of dealing effectively with the demands of the internal and external environments. Thus, this person perceives that he is loved by significant others (especially parents) and that he is worthy of this love. The individual with high self-esteem typically feels that he is at least as smart as his chronological age-mates, and generally reports that he is satisfied with his performance at school or work.

10

LOW SELF-ESTEEM

Individuals with low self-esteem:

1. tend to lack initiative and behave in a non-assertive fashion in their interactions with others.
2. tend to experience more intense symptoms of depression and anxiety than their counterparts with high self-esteem.
3. tend to worry a lot and possess pessimistic views regarding the future.
4. tend to be more timid, shy and predisposed to withdrawal than individuals who esteem themselves highly.
5. tend to be indecisive and usually vacillate when confronted with obstacles.
6. tend to be more prone to emitting self-defeating responses and developing self-punishing modes of behavior.

The individual with low self-esteem typically considers herself to be less capable than her peers, and generally possesses pessimistic views regarding her ability to exert a significant positive effect on her environment. The perceptions that individuals with low self-esteem possess regarding their personal worth are generally negative.

RESPONSES REFLECTING SELF-ESTEEM: HIGH AND LOW

The child with high self-esteem typically answers "yes" to the following statements incorporated in *The Culture-Free Self-Esteem Inventory for Children*, whereas the child with low self-esteem generally answers "no."

- I am happy most of the time.

- Boys and girls like to play with me.

- I can do things as well as other boys and girls.

Adults with high self-esteem typically answer "yes" to the following questions incorporated in *The Culture-Free Self-Esteem Inventory for Adults*, whereas the adult with low self-esteem typically answers "no."

- Are you happy most of the time?

- Can you do things as well as others?

- Do you feel you are as important as most people?

ACHIEVEMENT

Some individuals propose that *"As A Group Our Students Are Generally Experiencing Academic Deficits Because Our Teachers Emphasize The Enhancement of Self-Esteem Too Strongly."* Actually, the emphasis on self-esteem is a recent development. For instance, during February, 1987 I lectured at the annual conference of the *Self-Esteem Institute* in Santa Clara, California. This occasion was only the fourth conference held by the California group; the first national conference on self-esteem was held in October, 1987 in St. Louis, Missouri.

Early school leavers or school dropouts and under-achievement, or lack of satisfactory levels of academic achievement are problems that have plagued the field of education for many decades.

The problem of early school leavers is generally estimated to be approximately 30 percent among the general population of Canadians. However in a recent study *(September, 1993)* sponsored by *Employment and Immigration Canada,*

For Teachers, Parents and Kids:

statistics reported a dropout rate of 18 percent and estimated that 40 percent of the early school leavers were age sixteen or less when they dropped out of school and that 32 percent of them had grade nine education or less.

Students who drop out of school prior to obtaining their high school diplomas tend to experience greater economic problems than their counterparts who do not drop out. For instance, regarding economics, Kinisawa *(1988)* states that:

- 52 percent of dropouts are unemployed or receiving welfare
- 60 percent of prison inmates are high school dropouts
- 87 percent of pregnant teenagers are high school dropouts.

Similar findings are provided by Rumberger *(1987)*, who reported that the life time earnings of American males aged 16 to 64 who completed high school is $250,000 greater than the earnings of individuals in the same age group who did not complete high school.

Data derived from research studies *(e.g. Macdonald, 1988)* indicate that high school dropouts experience social problems with the general population and peers as well and are generally categorized as being losers. A significant proportion of youth who experience learning problems and school failure abuse alcohol and possess lower levels of self-esteem and have difficulties in their relationships with their parents. For instance, Yanish and Battle *(1985)* studied twenty-two youths who were experiencing behavioral problems and found that alcohol consumption in this group was significantly associated with academic problems and conflict in interpersonal interactions with parents.

In addition to economic, social and mental health difficulties, school dropouts generally experience academic problems as well. For instance, Radwanski *(1987)*, studied high school students in Ontario, Canada and found that 82 percent of early school leavers had failed at least one subject, whereas only 50 percent of those who graduated from high school had received failing grades. Although many school dropouts are low achievers, they generally possess average intellectual ability. However, they often become defeated or disturbed leavers who possess low self-esteem and lack confidence in their ability to perform academic tasks *(Battle, 1982; Depauw, 1987)*.

Radwanski *(1987)*, offers the following quotes provided by the school dropouts whom he studied in Ontario, Canada:

1. I just wanted to get out and get a feel for people who cared, and go where people could answer questions honestly. Not teachers who didn't care about students.

2. If you failed an exam, they dumped on you and they didn't show you where you went wrong. They treated me like a grade school kid.

3. I left school to find a job. To make money. Just to look for any job. Nothing specific at the time. I wasn't doing very good and was in trouble all the time. I was depressed because I wasn't doing very good.

4. I wish I had more contact with teachers. They teach a whole class instead of teaching individuals.

5. The teachers weren't there for me. I was an A student, but I didn't like their attitude. They didn't care.

6. I'm not smart, so the school system ignored me.

Early school-leavers or dropouts generally find it difficult to obtain and maintain employment and this problem appears to be escalating. For instance, Thomas *(1987)*, states that in 1950, high school dropouts were eligible for 34 percent of available jobs in the United States, whereas in 1987, early school leavers were capable of performing only 8 percent of available jobs. The predicament of high levels of unemployment for school dropouts deserves special attention because the individual who has less than average self-esteem, coupled with a relatively low level of education and no job, is at high risk for a lifetime of problems for the person himself and for his society.

UNDERACHIEVEMENT

The problems of underachievement and lack of achievement have plagued the field of education for generations. In my book entitled *"Enhancing Self-Esteem And Achievement,"* which was originally published in 1982, I said that:

> Investigators present different estimates of the number of underachievers, but generally agree that the percentage is high. For example, H.M. Alter *(1952)* in a study of 1,162 students living in high socioeconomic areas, found a total of 74 *(7 percent)* of a suburban junior-senior high school population to possess IQ scores of 130 or above on the *California Test of Mental Maturity (CTMM)*. He selected 45 of this group of 74 to study and found that 19 *(42 percent)* were severe underachievers.

> Other theorists *(e.g.; Wedemeyer 1953; Ritter and Thorn 1954; Coleman 1965; and Wolpe 1954)* state that between 20 and 50 percent of students work below their potential and, as a consequence may be classified as underachievers.

A review of research literature reveals that between 5 and 50 percent of students may be classified as underachievers. These figures however, should not be taken literally, because figures illustrating the degree of underachievement tend to vary from study to study, and are determined to a large extent by the particular method or technique employed to identify underachievers. Results, nevertheless, indicate that the problem is a profound one and that there is a critical need to implement procedures that assist our young people in developing their potential more effectively.

The findings listed above clearly indicate that underachievement and lack of achievement is a crucial problem that existed long before the self-esteem movement gained popularity.

My research *(Battle, 1993)* indicates that few schools in the United States and Canada have in operation formal self-esteem enhancement programs. Also of the few with self-esteem programs, only a small percentage of them assess the self-esteem of their students to determine if they are achieving desired results.

BEHAVIOR

Display of violent behavior by children and youth has escalated in recent years. For example, in Alberta, Canada, a province which is considered by most residents to be a peaceful nonviolent place to live, during 1992, a 16 year old killed his step father, mother and siblings; also during 1992, a junior high school student killed a peer at school and in 1994, three juveniles murdered a housewife in her home in the same province.

For Teachers, Parents and Kids:

The growth of youth gangs and the problem of "drive-by" shootings among North American teens has become a serious issue. Because of this, many educators and representatives of social service and corporate organizations feel that there is an important need to develop and implement programs intended to reduce the incidence of youth behaviors that impinges on the rights of others.

At a political level in Canada and the United States many residents are lobbying politicians to make amendments to the *Young Offenders Act* to ensure that youth who commit crimes be required to deal with consequences that are appropriate for their offenses. For instance, the proposed changes tabled by Canada's *Solicitor General* during May, 1994 calls for longer sentences for youth who commit violent crimes. The proposed amendments to the *Young Offenders Act* also makes it easier for young offenders aged 12 to 17 to be tried in adult court.

Display of inappropriate behavior by school age children is an important issue which some professional educators and elected trustees consider to be the number one problem in their districts. These observations have prompted some school jurisdictions to employ Behavioral Consultants to assist students in managing their behavior more appropriately. Also, in some districts students who display persistent inappropriate behavior are diagnosed by school psychologists as being Severe Behavior Disordered and are provided with special needs programs intended to assist them in managing their behavior more appropriately. Moreover, some districts have established special classes and special schools for students who display behavior that is judged to be inappropriate and in some instances, dangerous, to the welfare of the student who displays the deviant behavior, his or her classmates and teachers.

Oppositional Deviant Disorder

Oppositional Defiant Disorder is a fairly common behavior problem of children and youth. Oppositional Defiant Behavior is characterized by negative, hostile and deviant behavior towards parents and other authority figures. Children who are experiencing Oppositional Defiant Behavior typically are argumentative with adults, frequently lose their temper, swear and often are angry, resentful and easily annoyed by others.

The following case of Phyllis prepared by Meyer, Hardaway-Osborne *(1982)* illustrates common behaviors displayed by adolescents experiencing Oppositional Deviant Disorder.

Case Report 1:1
Phyllis: Oppositional Deviant Behavior.

Throughout Phyllis' childhood, her parents were United States Embassy officials in several South American countries. When Phyllis entered high school, her parents moved back to the States and joined the political science department of a small private college. Phyllis attended public high school for two years and was suspended four times. Her parents enrolled her in a private girls' academy, hoping the structured atmosphere would "settle her down." However, Phyllis was suspended from the academy twice in the first semester, and the principal had threatened permanent expulsion if her school behavior did not improve. The school had a weekly "detention hall" for students who had broken rules. Phyllis' suspensions resulted primarily from noncompliance with detention hall and the sheer number of outstanding detentions. The infractions for which she received detention were generally minor, such as talking during class, violations of dress code, and tardiness for detention hall.

Phyllis, the youngest of five girls, was the only daughter who still lived with her parents at the time she was referred by her school's guidance counsellor to a clinical psychologist. Phyllis' married sisters lived in other states and were employed as nurse, kindergarten teacher, medical technologist, and engineer respectively. There were four years separating Phyllis and the next youngest sister (medical technologist). Phyllis' parents described the family as close and loving. They said that the older girls had gone through brief periods of rebellion during adolescence but that they all grew out of it. The family was very achievement-oriented, and everyone except Phyllis had distinguished academic records.

Phyllis had behaved normally through childhood, though she had been very stubborn and difficult at the age of three years old and had often been prone to temper tantrums, causing her father to semi-affectionately dub her as "the little witch." Phyllis had always produced an inconsistent academic performance. Throughout grammar school, she often earned above-average grades, yet her teachers consistently concluded that Phyllis' potential was higher than her grades indicated. Junior high school was characterized by a particularly erratic performance. Phyllis received her first failing grade in seventh grade, and from then on would fail one or two subjects each grading period. Her parents would restrict her privileges and closely supervise Phyllis' homework in the failed subject(s). In subsequent grading periods, Phyllis would earn high marks in the previously failed subject(s) only to fail a different subject. After transferring to the academy, Phyllis' overall performance level improved, though it remained inconsistent.

Similar inconsistencies were observed in Phyllis' social relationships. She had several "personality conflicts" with teachers, on whom she blamed her low grades, and her parents described her as "moody and difficult to get along with" as she neared adolescence. At home, frequent arguments erupted over Phyllis' grades and her failure to complete household chores. When the tension in the home became intolerable, Phyllis would visit one of her sisters. However, these visits were often prematurely terminated by some disagreement with her sister or brother-in-law concerning Phyllis' curfew.

In grade school, Phyllis apparently got along fairly well with her classmates. The family moved every two or three years, however, and Phyllis had not continued any of her childhood friendships. In high school, she moved from one close girlfriend to another, often within a few weeks. These friendships seemed to die from lack of interest on the girls' parts and seldom resulted in an actual argument. Phyllis dated frequently but did not have a steady boyfriend. This was an additional source of conflict in the family, since her mother suspected, without any hard evidence, that Phyllis was sexually active. (pp. 31-32).

Source: Meyer, R.G. and Hardaway - Osborne, Y.U., 1982. *Case Studies in Abnormal Behavior*, Boston: Allyn and Bacon. *Reprinted by permission of the publisher.*

For Teachers, Parents and Kids:

A significant percentage of educators propose that undesirable behavior which often results in conflicts among students is increasing. Quantitative support for this position is provided by Battle *(1993)* in his most recent standardization of *The Culture-Free Self-Esteem Inventory For Children-Form A, 2,* in which he found that the mean social self-esteem (examinee's perceptions of his interpersonal relationships with peers) score of the children who participated in the studies have declined.

Battle *(1994)* in his comparative analysis of the social self-esteem scores of elementary level students who participated in the initial standardization of the CFSEI with those who participated in the most recent studies found that the children in the initial studies *(Battle, 1981)* earned a mean social self-esteem score of 7.1, whereas the value for those who participated in the most recent studies *(Battle, 1993)* was 6.05. It is also important to note that the boys and girls who participated in the most recent studies earned mean self-esteem scores that were higher in academic (previous mean = 7.0; current mean = 7.52) , and parent (previous mean = 7.4; current mean = 7.7) facets of self-esteem. The decline in social self-esteem (previous mean = 7.1; current mean = 6.05) provide support for those educators who rate student behavior as a major problem confronting educators in North American schools.

PURPOSE AND BEHAVIOR

I am of the opinion that insights regarding behavior and its purpose can be used to assist teachers and parents in their attempts to promote the self-esteem, academic achievement and behavioral self-control of the children they serve.

We support the view which proposes that all human behavior has purpose and is goal-directed. We recognize that an individual may not be aware of the motives compelling his or her behavior; but we nevertheless feel that in every instance behavior is guided or directed by some underlying purpose. This position is vividly illustrated by Adler *(1927, p. 29)* in the following passage:

> Psychic life of man is determined by his goal. No human being can think, feel, will, dream, without all these activities being determined, continued, modified and directed toward an ever present objective....A real understanding of the behavior of any human being is impossible without a clear comprehension of the secret goal which he is pursuing.

BIRTH ORDER AND BEHAVIOR

The idea that birth order influences behavior is not a new one. It dates back to Galton *(1874)*, who proposed that birth order was an important factor affecting the contributions of English scientists *(Miley 1969, p. 64)*. More recent theorists *(most notably Adler, 1927)* believe that one's ordinal position in the family exerts a strong effect on one's perception of self-worth and behavior. Adler communicated his emphasis on the importance of birth order when he said, "Above all, we must rid ourselves of the superstition that the situation within the family is the same for each individual child."

Adler thought that, although siblings live in the same home setting, they do not experience identical social environments because they are not treated in exactly the same fashion by parents and significant others. The first born, for instance, typically receives a tremendous amount of parental attention until the second child comes along. When the second child is born, the oldest feels "dethroned," and as a consequence typically starts to misbehave in an attempt to recapture his former position as the center of attention of parents. The first born, however, cannot succeed, because the younger child needs considerable attention. As a result of this inevitable "dethroning" experience, the oldest child is often oriented toward the past, pessimistic about the future, and prone to develop emotional problems. In addition, the oldest child tends to be conscientious, conservative, responsible and compliant.

The second born is typically a more secure child because he or she does not experience the traumatic "dethronement" that the first born must endure. Resulting from his ordinal position, the second born often experiences pressure from both sides (from the oldest and from the youngest), and as a consequence frequently develops highly competitive modes of behaving which often enables him to develop at a faster rate than the first born child. It is often observed that second born children tend to speak at an earlier age than first borns. Adler felt that the second born child was the one most likely to develop favorably.

The youngest child is typically an ambitious, high achieving individual who generally attempts to surpass older siblings. If the youngest child is spoiled or pampered, however, he frequently displays inadequacy and assumes that others should take care of his personal needs. Because parents tend to spoil the youngest child, these children may experience difficulties due to an unwillingness to work up to potential. The youngest child frequently behaves like a helpless individual who is incapable of doing things independently.

In families in which there are more than three children, proponents of Adlerian psychology generally agree that children will display variable behavior. For instance, the third child in a family of four children would probably behave like a middle child, whereas the second child in a family of this size may display the type of behavior one would otherwise expect of the oldest child.

The only child is of course the first born; but unlike the oldest child, this child does not experience "dethronement" and loss of prominence. The only child is the focus of parents' attention and, as a consequence of this attention, often matures earlier than is typical of first born children. This attention can have a negative affect on the only child's value development because he runs the risk of overvaluing personal worth and having unrealistic expectations regarding the amount of attention he should receive. When the only child enters school, for instance, he often finds it difficult to understand why he cannot be the center of the teacher's attention. The only child's egocentricity often results in behavioral problems and strained relationships with other pupils - frequently resulting in ostracism by peers. Adler felt that only children tend to be timid and dependent, and generally possess lower-than-average social interest because they find it difficult to concern themselves with the needs of others.

Other writers (*e.g., Coopersmith 1967; Rosenberg 1965; Schutz 1983*) also propose that birth order is related to self-esteem. Coopersmith found that first born and only children earned higher self-esteem scores, and Rosenberg found that only children earned higher self-esteem scores than average. Schultz studied 542 fifth-grade students and found a significant relationship between birth order and social self-esteem as measured by *The Culture-Free Self-Esteem Inventory For Children (Battle 1981)*, with the relationship being the strongest for middle children.

Although some experts, such as Adler, assume that birth order is a major variable affecting behavior, we think that perception is the most important variable affecting behavior. These positions are not so contradictory as they may seem, however. How parents interact with their children in light of ordinal birth position affects the child's perception of self-worth, which in turn determines his or her characteristic mode of behaving.

Understanding Misbehavior

Although children, and teenagers too, prefer to obtain their purposes by cooperating or behaving "appropriately," some feel compelled to manifest misbehavior, which generally impedes self-esteem and parents' attempts to assist their children in developing their potential. Misbehavior, like behavior in general, has purpose and goals. Keeping in mind that the person may not be aware of the purpose or goal, we see children misbehave when their interactions with people significant to them are negative and when they are discouraged.

The most commonly quoted goals of children's misbehaving are those noted by Dreikurs *(1971)*. Dreikurs enumerated the four goals of children's misbehaving: 1) attention, 2) power, 3) revenge, and 4) display of inadequacy.

Attention

The desire for attention is almost universal in children. Children prefer to obtain attention by behaving in a cooperative, positive fashion; however, if they cannot get the attention they desire by behaving positively, they will emit negative behavior in these attempts. For example, if a child with a learning disability cannot get the teacher's attention by performing well academically, he or she may seek attention by misbehaving. Thus, children experiencing learning disabilities often develop behavioral problems. For another example, when a child refuses to go to bed, she is generally wanting attention. When she annoys her parents by insisting on a snack, then a drink of water and, after these, permission to use the bathroom, attention is the sought-for goal.

POWER

When the child's goal of misbehaving is power, he generally attempts to demonstrate to parents and other adults that they can't make him do anything that he doesn't want to do. Children seeking power feel that they are significant only when they are "the boss" therefore, they may refuse to cooperate and frequently involve themselves in power struggles in their interactions with peers, parents, and other adults (e.g., teachers). The child displaying a bid for power may be overtly defiant in his interactions with others or resist passively. The latter, covert negativism, can be conveyed subtly when the child appears to be compliant, but nonetheless refuses to do what adults want him to do. Any teacher or parent who has heard, "I'll do it in a minute," only to find the requested task never performed, has experienced a child wielding power.

REVENGE

Children who pursue revenge are hurt; as a consequence, they want to hurt others. Children who are seeking revenge feel that they have been mistreated by those important to them (e.g., parents), and strive to "get even" with those they feel are responsible for the mistreatment. In their attempts to retaliate, for example, many of such children underachieve; if achievement is an important goal

For Teachers, Parents and Kids:

of parents for their children, this is an effective way of disappointing those expectations. Similarly, adolescents who are seeking revenge often act their feelings out sexually and get deeply involved in drugs in order to hurt parents they feel have mistreated them.

The following case of Kathy is offered to illustrate how adolescents pursuing revenge often behave.

CASE REPORT 1:2
KATHY; 15 YEARS, 8 MONTHS.

Kathy, who was adopted when she was two months old, was the youngest child in a family with three children. Kathy's early development was generally normal. She walked at 10 months, started to use sentences at 17 months, and was toilet trained at 2 years, 4 months.

Kathy entered kindergarten at age four and a half and first grade when she was five. Kathy was a "model" student during the elementary school years, an honor student who was placed in a "gifted" class when she was in fifth grade. Her behavior was generally positive until her teen years. Kathy's problems began to manifest themselves when she was 12 and in the eighth grade.

Kathy reported, "When I turned 12, I started to hate my stepfather", but she didn't provide an explanation for this sudden onset of dislike for him. Until this point, she had been her dad's favorite daughter, and they had generally enjoyed a very positive relationship. At this time of onset, Kathy's relationship with her stepmother was more positive than with her stepfather; but they experienced difficulties because Kathy felt her mother was an unaffectionate person who was too strict and punitive. During the eighth-grade year Kathy started to use drugs, underachieve, and have sexual intercourse with numerous boys. She got into fights on several occasions at school; and, as a consequence of her misbehavior, she was subsequently placed in a private school when she was 13. Her behavior was so deviant in this setting that she was expelled two years later. At age 15 Kathy's stepmother referred her to a psychologist for assessment and treatment. The psychologist found Kathy to be a very bright youngster. Her Verbal, Performance, and Full Scale IQ scores on the *Wechsler Intelligence Scale For Children* were 115, 135, and 128 respectively. The psychologist diagnosed Kathy as being an adolescent who was experiencing a "conduct disorder, undersocialized aggressive type," and provided her with psychotherapy. According to the psychologist, the goal of Kathy's misbehavior was revenge intended to hurt parents who she felt put conditions on their love for her and who set unrealistically high expectations for her that were, in her view, unattainable. Although some gains were made during psychotherapy, she continued to misbehave. Because of her persistent misbehavior, Kathy was placed in a group home for juvenile delinquents.

DISPLAY OF INADEQUACY

Children who display inadequacy or disability, attempt to convince others that they can't do things. They often present themselves as being dumb, incapable, hopeless. These maneuvers, however, are manipulative and are representative of the child's attempt to get others to do things for him or her.

The following case of Tommy provides a typical illustration of a child displaying inadequacy.

CASE REPORT 1:3
TOMMY; 12 YEARS, 5 MONTHS.

Tommy was the youngest child, the only boy in a family of four children. His parents were middle-aged, and he was ten years younger than his sister closest in age to him. Tommy's development during his first six years was within normal limits. He walked at 12 months, started using sentences at 20 months, and was toilet trained at 2 years, 10 months.

Tommy was enrolled in kindergarten at the age of four and a half. Kindergarten was a good year for Tommy, and he functioned quite well in first and second grade. He started to experience academic difficulty in the third grade, however, and continued to experience problems throughout the elementary years and grades seven and eight. Because of Tommy's persistent academic problems, his parents joined the local chapter of parents of children with learning disabilities because they assumed that he "had a learning disability." Tommy's teachers generally reported that he was having difficulties in reading and spelling, but that he enjoyed arithmetic and performed fairly well in that area. His teachers also generally reported that they felt Tommy could earn better grades; and his fifth- and sixth-grade teachers recommended that he repeat; but his parents refused to let him repeat because they felt repeating would exert a negative effect on his self-esteem.

When Tommy was failing eighth grade, his parents referred him to a psychologist. The psychologist administered an IQ test to Tommy and found him to be a bright youngster with Verbal, Performance, and Full Scale IQ scores of 109, 115 and 113 respectively, on the *Wechsler Intelligence Scale for Children.* The psychologist diagnosed Tommy as an egocentric child who was underachieving and "displaying inadequacy." The psychologist recommended that Tommy's parents and teachers cooperate closely and ensure that he would make an "appropriate" effort before giving up on a task. They were told that, if he did not complete tasks that he was capable of completing during regularly scheduled periods, he should be required to do them during his free periods or at home after school.

After this recommended structure was implemented, Tommy made significant academic progress:

TEST	GRADE SCORE JUNE 1979	GRADE SCORE FEB. 1980	GRADE SCORE AUG. 1980
Schonell Reading	4.4	5.6	6.6
Schonell Spelling	3.5	5.2	5.5
Schonell Comp	4.5	7.8	9.2
Bett's Vocab	4.5	6.1	6.2
Monroe-Sherman	5.5	5.8	9.8

IDENTIFYING MISBEHAVIOR

Parents and other adults can identify the goals of children's misbehavior by identifying how they feel when the children misbehave. Two popular contemporary psychologists, Dinkmeyer and McKay *(1976)*, propose that parents and other adults tend to feel annoyed when the children's goal of misbehavior is attention; angry, when the child's goal is power; hurt, when the child's goal is revenge; and they feel like giving up in despair when the child's goal is a display of inadequacy *(Battle, 1990, pp. 14 - 20)*.

RIGHTS

It is important to realize that in our democratic society, children, parents and teachers have rights.

In 1970, the *Joint Commission on the Mental Health of Children (1970, pp 3-4)* listed the following seven rights that all babies are born with:

1. to be wanted

2. to be born healthy

3. to live in a healthy environment

4. to satisfaction of basic needs

5. to continuous loving care

6. to acquire intellectual and emotional skills enabling them to achieve their aspirations and cope in society

7. to receive care and treatment

CHILDREN'S RIGHTS

Tolor and Deigan *(1984)* propose that the following are rights of children:

1. Children have the right to be provided for in regards to their physical and emotional needs.

2. Children have the right to be protected from physical or emotional abuse.

3. Children have the right to feel secure and safe.

4. Children have the right to receive all necessary health care.

5. Children have the right to obtain increasing privileges as their age increases.

6. Children have the right to learn through their own experiences.

7. Children have the right to keep personal thoughts to themselves.

8. Children have the right to their privacy.

9. Children have the right to their own fantasies.

10. Children have the right to expect that others will not examine their possessions, notes, letters, diaries, etc., without permission.

11. Children have the right to feel negatively as well as positively toward others, including parents.

12. Children have the right occasionally to take time to do absolutely nothing.

13. Children have the right to express opinions contrary to their parents' opinion.

14. Children have the right to participate in decision-making about matters that concern them, such as their clothing, people they associate with, and activities they engage in.

15. Children have the right to complain.

16. Children have the right to be seen and heard.

17. Children have the right to be children, meaning that they are not expected to act as miniature adults.

18. Children have the right to have fun.

19. Children have the right to quarrel with siblings and other children.

20. Children have the right to have their discussions with health service providers kept confidential.

21. Children have the right to an appropriate education consistent with their needs *(pp. 139 - 140)*.

PARENT'S RIGHTS

Tolor and Deigan *(1984)* propose that the following are rights of parents:

1. Parents have the right to have a variety of feelings toward their children.
2. Parents have the right to say "no" to their children.
3. Parents have the right to have a life apart from their children.
4. Parents have the right to express their own needs and their ways of looking at issues to their children.
5. Parents have the right to expect children to assume increasing responsibility as they grow older.
6. Parents have the right to their privacy.
7. Parents have the right to express their values to their children.
8. Parents have the right to protect and preserve their health, which means that there is a limit to what they can or should do for their children.
9. Parents have the right to be away from their children at times.
10. Parents have the right to set limits on their children's behavior.
11. Parents have the right to be concerned about their children.
12. Parents have the right to take precautionary measures to keep their children from harming themselves or others.
13. Parents have the right to determine whether their children are obtaining an appropriate education and to use legal means to work towards the fulfillment of the child's educational needs.

For Teachers, Parents and Kids:

TEACHER'S RIGHTS

Tolar and Deigan *(1984)* propose that the following are rights of teachers:

1. Teachers have the right to be concerned for the children they teach.

2. Teachers have the right to learn.

3. Teachers have the professional right to seek the welfare of the children in their care.

4. Teachers have the right to receive appropriate remuneration for their work.

5. Teachers have the right to ask for and receive administrative and professional help in educating a child with exceptional learning or emotional needs.

6. Teachers have the right to participate in educational decisions concerning the children in their care.

7. Teachers have the right to pursue a life apart from their professional responsibilities.

8. Teachers have the right to be informed of any issues which are critical to that child's education.

9. Teachers have the right to be professionally creative in their teaching.

10. Teachers have the right to meet and interact with parents.

11. Teachers have the right to be respected members of the professional community *(pp. 141 - 142).*

Summary

1. Self-esteem, achievement and behavior are crucial variables that affect the lives of all individuals.

2. Emphasis on self-esteem is a recent development.

3. Self-esteem is a fundamental need and one of the most important variables affecting the lives of individuals at all stages of development.

4. Self-esteem refers to the perception the individual possesses of his/her own worth.

5. Self-esteem is a subjective construct which is strongly tied to personality.

6. Individuals with high self-esteem tend to be more effective in meeting environmental demands.

7. Individuals with low self-esteem tend to lack initiative and behave in a non-assertive fashion in their interactions with others.

8. Self-esteem and achievement are interrelated.

9. Early school leavers or school dropouts tend to experience low levels of self-esteem.

10. Alcohol consumption is significantly associated with academic problems and conflict in interpersonal interactions with parents.

11. Underachievement among school age children is a serious problem.

12. Display of violent behavior by children and youth has escalated in recent years.

13. Social self-esteem is a major problem of contemporary youth.

14. Behavior has purpose, and all of us are influenced mostly by social forces.

15. Birth order is an important factor influencing behavior because it affects one's perception of self-worth.

16. Children misbehave and there are identifiable goals of these misbehaviors.

17. Children, parents and teachers have rights.

PART II

Promotion &
Enhancement Strategies

CHAPTER 2

Strategies That Enhance Kid's Self-Esteem and Achievement

IN THIS CHAPTER, WE DESCRIBE STRATEGIES that teachers and parents can use to enhance the self-esteem and academic achievement of the children they serve. Enhancement of self-esteem, as I vision it, is a growth oriented process which is strongly affected by perception, which in turn influences behavior.

PERCEPTION AND BEHAVIOR

I am of the opinion that teachers and parents should familiarize themselves with the role that perception plays in behavior in the early stages of their attempts to enhance the self-esteem and academic levels of the children they serve. The group of psychologists who have directed the most energy toward studying the role that perception plays are commonly called phenomenologists. Phenomenologists stress subjective perception and propose that the individual reacts to the world in terms of his unique perception of it. Hence, perception is the most important variable determining behavior. The following case, that of Bob, illustrates the role that perception of self plays on behavior.

CASE REPORT 2.1

Bob was an average seventeen-year-old senior attending a small midwestern high school. Near the end of his senior year, Bob and other graduating seniors journeyed to the university to take college entrance examinations. Bob earned average scores on his examination, but a computer error assigned him a score at the 95th percentile. When Bob's test results reached the school, his principal was shocked to discover that Bob had earned the highest score in his school and was among the top two percent in the entire state. He found this particularly difficult to accept, because he and the faculty had always viewed Bob as being an average student. The principal, nevertheless reassessed his perceptions of Bob and started to view him as being a very capable student. When the results were viewed by the counsellor, he reassessed his perceptions of Bob, and assumed that the average standardized test scores Bob had earned throughout the years, apparently, were not valid indicators of his true level of potential. When Bob's results were observed by his homeroom teacher, she reassessed her views of Bob. When she informed Bob's parents of his score, they started to view him differently. After observing the way his principal, counsellor, teacher and parents were reacting toward him, Bob reassessed his perceptions of himself and started to see himself as not merely being "average" but quite capable. Subsequently, Bob became one of the highest achievers of his era. He is now a practicing physician.

Perception is the major determinant of behavior and in most cases (as in the case of Bob) determines whether or

For Teachers, Parents and Kids:

not an individual makes significant or routine contributions to his society; how we view ourselves determines how we respond to the demands of our environment.

Adults (e.g., parents, teachers) perceptions regarding the self-esteem and adjustment states of school-age children generally determine their placements. However, occasionally the perceptions that adults possess regarding children's subjective states are not congruent with what the children are actually experiencing. In a series of comprehensive studies, children residing in six different countries enrolled in grades three through nine were asked to rate 20 different life events on a scale ranging from 7 (the most upsetting experience), to 1 (the least upsetting). Findings derived from these series of studies indicate that the children rated the 20 life events almost identically, although they came from different cultures and different ethnic backgrounds. The ratings from these studies are presented in Table 2:1.

Data in Table 2:1 indicates that a "culture of childhood" exists in which children in different countries tend to see things similarly. Moreover, this data indicates that what adults consider to be stressful for children is quite incongruent with what the children consider to be stressful. For example, if parents and teachers consider "wetting" in class to be nonstressful to the child, and having a new baby in the family to be quite stressful, their perceptions are quite incongruent with those of the child.

TABLE 2:1: CHILDREN'S RATING OF THE DEGREE OF UPSET OF EXPERIENCES (GRADES 3 THROUGH 9)		
LIFE EVENT	U.S.A.	JAPAN
1. Losing a parent	6.90	6.90
2. Going blind	6.86	6.68
3. Held back a grade	6.82	6.78
4. Wetting in class	6.74	6.73
5. Parents fighting	6.71	6.23
6. Caught in a theft	6.63	6.73
7. Suspected of lying	6.53	6.73
8. A poor report card	6.23	6.61
9. Sending to principal	5.75	6.63
10. Having an operation	5.51	5.82
11. Getting lost	5.59	5.01
12. Ridiculed in class	5.28	6.11
13. Move to a new school	4.60	5.21
14. Scary dream	4.08	5.07
15. Not making 100 on a test	3.75	5.04
16. Picked last on team	3.30	5.92
17. Losing in a game	3.16	4.48
18. Going to the dentist	2.73	3.05
19. Giving a class report	2.58	2.75
20. New baby sibling	1.27	1.43
Source: *Journal of Child Psychology and Psychiatry*, Vol. 28, No. 6		

Because perceptions exert such a strong influence on behavior, it is important for teachers and other caregivers to realize that children's perceptions of events may differ from those of adults. Also, it is important for teachers and other caretakers to realize that a student's perception of her relationship with them influences the behavior she displays. This occurs in every instance, whether the student's behavior is congruent or incongruent with objective reality.

CAN TEACHERS ENHANCE
SELF-ESTEEM AND ACHIEVEMENT?

Teachers can augment the self-esteem and achievement patterns of their pupils *(Battle, 1981, 1982, 1993)*. Teachers can exert this effect because once the child enters school, teachers function "in loco parentis", sharing many of the responsibilities of parents. Consequently, when children enter school, teachers become the most significant other affecting the self-esteem of their pupils. Support for this position is provided by W.D. Labenne and B.I. Green *(1969)*. They stress the important role teachers play in the formation of their pupils' perceptions of self-worth when they state, "Any person who is intimately involved in the administration of rewards and punishments is in a position to become a significant other; it is not merely the ability or responsibility of administering the system...that makes a teacher a significant other. Rather, it is the manner in which she uses her authority that causes her to have a potent impact *(pp. 27)*."

Teachers exert a powerful influence on their pupils' self-esteem. Thus, how teachers interact with their pupils significantly affects students' perceptions of self-worth. Staines *(1958)*, found that teachers who interacted positively with their pupils induced positive changes in their students' self-esteem; whereas teachers who did not interact positively with their pupils induced negative shifts in the self-esteem of their students.

J. Canfield and H.C. Wells *(1976)* state:

It is possible to change self-concepts, and it is possible for teachers to effect the changes - either way both positive and negative. Many of us teach because we had a teacher or two who really had a significant impact on us. The impact was related to our self-concept. The teacher somehow communicated a sense of caring and a sense of our own personal worth. On the other hand, many of us have also experienced a teacher who humiliated us or our classmates through sarcasm and ridicule. These teachers made learning a negative experience. Teachers can and do affect pupils' self-concepts every day. You have a choice over what kind of effects you will have *(pp.4)*.

THE TEACHER AS CHILD ADVOCATE

Teachers should function as advocates for their pupils. As child advocates, teachers should help each child develop his/her potential to the fullest. To accomplish this very difficult task, it is essential that teachers attend to both cognitive and affective needs of developing children and youth. Thus, in addition to facilitating the development of cognitive abilities, teachers must also promote the development of positive perceptions of self-worth in their pupils.

In recent years some writers in the field of self-esteem have proposed that certain activities are required to enhance self-esteem. I propose that self-esteem, like personality, develops early in life (e.g. during the first 6 years), and is a consequence of early interactions with significant others (e.g. parents). Thus, in my view, the child brings her self-esteem with her when she enters school on the first day. Therefore, I'm of the opinion that what she needs to build her self-esteem, if it is lacking, are positive interactions that were available but were not provided during the developmental years by her parents or parent surrogates. The activities proposed by many writers may be beneficial,

For Teachers, Parents and Kids:

but they alone will not enhance self-esteem. For them to be beneficial they must be provided in concert with positive interactions that build self-esteem initially during the developmental process including unconditional positive regard, mutual respect and encouragement. The most important of these is unconditional positive regard. If parents or parent surrogates (i.e. teachers who function in loco parentis) provide their students a high degree of unconditional positive regard they will develop positive self-esteem.

The need for teachers to attend to and develop, both cognitive and affective aspects of developing children and youth is becoming increasingly more apparent. Thus, administrators, psychologists, teachers and parents are finally realizing that if we are to develop a pupil's potential to the fullest and produce citizens capable of functioning productively in current and future generations, we must attend to the self-esteem needs of developing children and youth. This need was vividly delineated by A. Combs and D. Snygg *(1959)* when they stated:

> Since the self-concept is a function of experience, what happens to students during their time spent in the educational system must be of vital importance in the development of the phenomenal self. Probably no other agency in our society outside the family has a more profound effect on the development of the individual's concept of self.... If it is important that students learn to perceive themselves as liked, wanted, acceptable and responsible, then it follows that education must provide them with the kind of experiences which help them see themselves as such and avoid treating them in ways that destroy positive self-feelings *(pp. 277-278).*

The importance of the role the teacher plays in the development and maintenance of the self is vividly illustrated by J.W. Staines *(1958)* in his study of the responses and comments of classroom teachers and the influences that these responses and comments have on the self-concepts of their children. He hypothesized:

1. The self-concept is a learned structure growing mainly from comments made by other people and from inferences drawn by children out of their experiences in home, school and other social groups.
2. Consequently, teachers could make marked differences in the self-concepts of children with their comments on the child's performance, status and self-confidence.

Staines analyzed the responses and comments of a group of teachers and found that students with teachers who used democratic methods, made positive comments and gave consideration to the child's self-concept, made positive changes in self-concepts of their children; whereas marked psychological insecurity and maladjustment were found in the children whose teachers emphasized correctness and subject matter. Teachers who emphasized correctness and subject matter did not recognize the important role that perceptions of self, play in the educational process. Staines made the following comments in his discussion of the implications of his findings:

> The educational significance of the self is reaffirmed when it is realized that changes in the self picture are an inevitable part of both outcomes and conditions of learning in every classroom, whether or not the

For Teachers, Parents and Kids:

teacher is aware of them....It is clear that teaching methods can be adapted so that definite changes of the sought will occur in the self. The self can be deliberately produced by suitable teaching methods *(pp.109)*.

Comments and findings reported by experts in the field clearly indicate that parents and teachers exert strong influences on the self-esteem of the children under their care. Although parents exert the greatest effect on their children, once the child enters school, teachers become the most significant people affecting the self-esteem of their pupils.

Although empirical data are generally lacking regarding the effectiveness of many strategies which teachers assume are effective methods of enhancing the self-esteem of pupils, I feel that any procedure resulting in the development of a more positive teacher-pupil interactive process has the potential to enhance the self-esteem of participating pupils *(see page 87)*.

Some investigators have reported that pupils' perceptions of teachers' feelings toward them affects their self-perceptions and achievement. For instance, Helen H. Davidson and D. Lang *(1960)* studied 203 proficient readers enrolled in grades 4, 5 and 6, and found that subjects' perceptions of their teachers' feelings toward them correlated between favourable perceptions of teachers' feelings and academic achievement and, in turn classroom behavior. J.M. Pahordy *(1969)* states that teachers' feelings toward children will subsequently affect the child's ability to read. He suggests that this occurs in three steps:

1. A teacher believes a child will succeed or fail; she communicates this belief, either verbally or nonverbally, to the child.

2. The child begins to see himself as the teacher sees him.

3. The child's perceptions of his reading abilities are reinforced by association with actual performance.

Additional support for the position that teachers' perceptions affects pupils' perception of self is provided by H.V. Perkins *(1958)*, who studied fourth and sixth grade students and their teachers, and found that teachers' perceptions of children's self-concepts show a positive and significant relationship to the children's expressed self-concepts. Snygg and Combs *(1959)* in their text, entitled *Individual Behavior,* in discussing the role of the teacher in the development of the self- image stated:

> The learning of any skill or item of subject matter is accompanied by the formation of attitudes by the pupil towards the subject, towards school, towards his teacher, towards teachers in general, towards adults, towards society, and towards himself which may be desirable or undesirable. As a result, how the subject matter is taught may be even more important than what is taught *(pp. 240).*

I predict that there will be greater pressures placed on teachers in current and future generations to achieve expected results in both cognitive and affective (self-esteem) areas. The emphasis on the latter is clearly delineated in the following recommendations offered by the *California Task Force* to promote self-esteem and personal and social responsibility:

1. Every school district in California should adopt the promotion of self-esteem and personal and social responsibility as a clearly stated goal and integrate

For Teachers, Parents and Kids:

self-esteem in its total curriculum and inform all persons of its policies and procedures that value staff members and students, and serve to foster mutual respect, esteem and cooperation.

2. Course work in self-esteem should be required for credentials and as a part of ongoing in-service training for all educators. At least one course in the nature and development of self-esteem (in one's self and in one's students), should be required for credentials in teaching, counselling or administration, and for maintaining those credentials. School districts should develop and expand training in the development of self-esteem and personal and social responsibility as part of their ongoing staff development programs *(Battle, 1993, pp. 14-17)*.

I feel that every school should incorporate in its curriculum strategies intended to promote the self-esteem, academic achievement, personal and social responsibility of the students it serves *(Battle, 1992; 1993)*. The greatest challenge to educators, mental health workers, youth workers, politicians and other caregivers in the year 2000 will be to develop and implement an effective, comprehensive program of prevention designed to address learning, conduct and adjustment problems....The core construct of an effective preventive model, as I envision it, is self-esteem *(Battle, 1993, pp. 165)*.

WHY SHOULD TEACHERS ENHANCE SELF-ESTEEM?

Teachers should strive to enhance the self-esteem of their students because self-esteem is highly associated with achievement. Research findings support this assumption and indicate that children experiencing learning problems generally earned lower self-esteem scores than their counterparts who were not experiencing learning problems.

Self-esteem is a better predictor of academic success than measured intelligence. Support for this position is provided by Morse *(1963)* who stated that self-concept is a better predictor of classroom achievement than intelligence. Wattenberg and Clifford *(1964)* found that measures of self-concept at the beginning of kindergarten proved to be more predictive of reading achievement two-and-a-half years later than IQ did. Additional support for the position that assumes self-esteem is a better predictor of academic success than measured intelligence is provided by Smith *(1969)*, who found that the correlation between self-esteem and achievement was higher than the correlation between intelligence and achievement, and Jones and Grieneekz, *(1970)* who proposed that self-concept is the most effective and consistent predictor of academic achievement, even better than test scores.

Yaniw *(1983)* administered *The Culture-Free Self-Esteem Inventory, Form A*, to 716 junior high boys and girls and found a linear correlation between self-esteem and actual grades. That is, he found that the students who earned the lowest grades earned lower self-esteem scores, whereas those who earned the highest grades earned the highest self-esteem scores.

Recently, Wechsler *(1991)* found the correlation between the full scale IQ on the Wechsler Intelligence Scale for Children - Revised, 3, and grade point average to be .47, and the values for verbal IQ and performance IQ with grade point average to be .42 and .39 respectively.

For Teachers, Parents and Kids:

Yaniw *(1983)* found the correlation between actual grades and the academic self-esteem facet of *The Culture-Free Self-Esteem Inventory for Children, Form A*, to be .57 for Math; .59 for Language Arts; .60 for Science; and .61 for Social Studies; all higher than the correlations between *WISC-R, 3,* IQ's and grade point average.

CAN PARENTS ENHANCE SELF-ESTEEM AND ACHIEVEMENT?

Parents, like teachers, can augment the self-esteem and achievement patterns of their children. Parents can do this because they exert the most powerful influence on their children. Parents enhance their children's self-esteem and achievement when they provide them with unconditional positive regard, encouragement, structure and realistic expectations, effective instruction and mutual desirable behavior.

THE PARENTS ROLE AND SELF-ESTEEM

Of all influences, parents have the strongest effect on the self-esteem of their children; and the interaction between parent and child (the parent-child interactive process) is the most important variable affecting whether the children will develop high, low or intermediate levels of self-esteem.

In general, if parents communicate to their children that they love them unconditionally and interact with them in a nonpunitive fashion, children will develop high levels of self-esteem. However, if parents communicate to their children that their love for them has conditions placed upon it, children will develop low levels of self-esteem.

The roles that parents assume in the family constellation tend to exert differential effects on the self-esteem of boys and girls. For instance, if Mom assumes a dominant role, and the father a passive one, these dispositions tend to have a positive effect on the girl's self-esteem, but a negative effect on the boy's self-esteem. Conversely, if Dad assumes a dominant role and Mom a passive one, this tends to have a positive effect on the boy's self-esteem, but a negative effect on the girl's. If both parents interact in a democratic fashion, and assume equal amounts of authority and responsibility, these dispositions generally have positive effects on the self-esteem of both boys and girls. The reverse, of course, is equally true. If both parents are punitive and interact with their children in a autocratic fashion, this will have negative effects on the self-esteem of both boys and girls.

If children are accepted, approved and respected for what they are, they will most likely acquire attitudes of self-esteem and self-acceptance. But if the significant people in their lives belittle, blame and reject them, they are likely to evolve unfavourable self-attitudes. On the whole, social psychological research has supported the overall postulate that we hold the keys to one another's self-conceptions and identities *(Kitano, 1989)*.

The way in which parents interact with their children at home is twice as predictive of their children's success in school than is their family's social or economic status *(Walberg, 1984)*.

The role that parents play in the development of healthy self-esteem was delineated by Coopersmith *(1967)* when he said:

For Teachers, Parents and Kids:

The child apparently perceives and appreciates the attention and approval expressed by his mother (and father) and tends to view her as favouring and supportive. He also appears to interpret her interest and concern as an indication of his significance; basking in the signs of his personal importance, he comes to regard himself favourably. *This is success in its most personal expression - the concern, the attention, and the time of significant others (Coopersmith, 1967).*

Coopersmith found from his extensive research that parents who promote the development of healthy self-esteem in their children possess the following characteristics:

- the parents possess high levels of self-esteem
- the parents consistently show respect for their children's rights and opinions
- the parents clearly define limits on their children's behavior

Coopersmith *(1967)* found four conditions most often associated with high self-esteem in children. These are:

1. The child experiences full acceptance of thoughts, feelings and values of his or her being.

2. The child operates on a context of clearly defined and enforced limits that are fair, non-oppressive and negotiable, but the child is not given unrestricted freedom. In consequence, the child experiences a sense of security as well as a clear basis for evaluating his or her behavior. Further, the limits generally entail high standards as well as confidence that the child will be able to meet them.

3. The child experiences respect for his or her dignity as a human being. The parents take the child's needs and wishes seriously. The parents are willing to negotiate family rules within carefully drawn limits. In other words, authority, but not authoritarianism, is in operation. As an expression of this overall attitude, they are less inclined to resort to punitive discipline (and there tends to be less need for punitive discipline), and more inclined to put the emphasis on rewarding and reinforcing positive behavior. The parents show an interest in the child, his or her social and academic life, and they are generally available for discussion when and as the child desires it.

4. The parents themselves tend to enjoy a high level of self-esteem. Since the way we treat others generally reflects the way we treat ourselves, this last finding is hardly surprising.

Rogers *(1951)*, provided support for the notion that parents are most important in the development of self-esteem in their children, when he stated that parents should provide their children with unconditional positive regard rather than conditional positive regard. Rogers urges parents to let their child know that he is loved, accepted and wanted, simply because "he is who he is," and that this prizing, loving, caring-for, is not conditional or dependent on the behavior the child emits *(Battle, 1982, pp. 31-32)*.

A.T. Jersild *(1960)* stated that self-discovery is a continuous process which affects achievement, and that significant others, especially parents, play the major role in the development of perceptions of self. His position is presented in the following comments:

For Teachers, Parents and Kids:

Among the earliest experiences which influence the development of the child's view of himself are those with other people....If a child is accepted, approved, respected, and liked for what he is, he will be helped to acquire an attitude of self-acceptance and respect himself. But if the significant people in his life - at first his parents and later his teachers, peers and other persons who wield an influence - belittle him, blame him and reject him, the growing child's attitudes toward himself are likely to become unfavourable. As he is judged by others, he will tend to judge himself *(pp. 123)*.

The role that parents play in the development of children's perceptions of self was identified by D. Snygg and A.W. Combs *(1959)*, and is reflected in the following passage taken from their book entitled *Individual Behavior:*

Out of interaction of the child with the world about him, the individual comes to differentiate more and more clearly his phenomenal self. Obviously, this concept can be only a function of the way he is treated by those who surround him. As he is loved or respected, praised or punished, fails or is able to compete, he becomes gradually to regard himself as important or unimportant, adequate or inadequate.... The child can see himself only in terms of his experiences and in terms of the treatment he receives from those responsible for his development. Since the phenomenal self is the result of experience, his behavior can only be an outgrowth of the meaning of that experience, and he must necessarily become in truth, what he has been labeled by the community which surrounds him *(pp. 83)*.

The important statement written by William Jeffries vividly illustrates the important role that parents play in the development of self-esteem in their children:

My father knew all my faults, but to hear him talk (and in my presence, at that), you would think I had few equals. He showed me in a hundred ways that he approved of me. When I disappointed him, he never showed anger, but instead assured me that he knew I would do better next time, that I could do great things. Every one should have one person somewhere in his life like my father.

The following poem summarizes my views of my parents whom I love so very much:

MY MOM AND DAD

Of all the people in my life,

My mom and dad made the greatest sacrifice.

My mom and dad were a wonderful pair,

Who provided me unconditional love,
    support and care.

They made things clear to me so that
    I could see,

The positive things in you and me.

They taught me how to work and plan,

To think of myself and respect
    my fellowman.

I thank my parents for how I see,

My views of the world, life, you and me.

WHO IS RESPONSIBLE
FOR STUDENT ACHIEVEMENT?

Research at the *Carnegie Foundation for the Advancement of Teaching* surveyed a group of teachers and found that 90 percent of those questioned felt that lack of parental support was a problem in their schools which impeded the academic progress of students *(January, 1989)*. A fairly equal percentage of parents generally blame teachers for the learning problems their children experience at school. These diverse views make the question of responsibility for learning relevant. I am of the opinion that teachers are basically responsible for the learning of students in the elementary, junior high and senior high years. Obviously, student learning progresses most favourably when both parents and teachers work cooperatively in their joint attempts to assist the student. However, teachers are paid professionals who should in my view, be mandated to obtain desired results (e.g. reasonable rates of learning on the part of students), while instructing pupils. I recommend that teachers develop a letter such as the one that follows in their attempts to promote cooperative interactions with parents:

The purpose of this correspondence is to introduce myself and state that I'm the home room teacher for your daughter/son —————. I look forward to working with you cooperatively throughout the school year in our joint efforts to assist your child in learning effectively. I invite you to contact me if you have questions, suggestions, desire information or just want to communicate.

Sincerely,

INTERACTIONS AND SELF-ESTEEM

The interactive process is most important in enhancing the self-esteem of students. Therefore, how the teacher interacts with her students is the most important variable affecting her students' self-esteem. Support for this position is provided by Staines *(1958)*, who found that teachers who interacted with their students in a positive fashion and attended to both cognitive and affective (self-esteem) needs of their students enhanced their pupils' self-esteem and achievement levels. He *(Staines, 1958)*, also found that when teachers attended only to the cognitive needs of their students their pupils' self-esteem decreased and they learned at a slower rate.

Specific activities are an important part of an effective self-esteem enhancement program. However, the interactive strategies that teachers apply on a daily basis are most important. Support for this position is provided from quantitative data derived from a series of studies conducted at an inner city community school *(Battle, 1990, pp. 297-300)*.

During the 1987-88 school year teachers at this community school were provided self-esteem inservices in which they were taught how to incorporate the interactive strategies of mutual respect, unconditional regard, encouragement and reflective listening in their daily instructional formats. During this school year *(1987-88)*, the students at the school experienced positive shifts in their self-esteem between pre-testing (total mean score=34.20) and post-testing (total mean score=36.19). During the 1989-90 school year eight of the nine teachers who taught at this school during the 1987-88 school year moved to other schools. The teachers who replaced them did not attend

For Teachers, Parents and Kids:

self-esteem inservices, but their students were provided the same program of activities (i.e., The Breakfast Program, The Nutrition Program, The Concert Program, The Police In-School Program, The Senior Citizens Drop-In Centre, The Summer Camping Program, Cultural Visitations and Interchange, The English as a Second Language Program, and Awards Ceremonies), to which they were exposed during the 1987-88 school year. The total pre-test mean self-esteem score for the students at this community school during September, 1989 was 34.01, whereas the value observed during post-testing which occurred during June of 1990 was 34.02. The total pre-test mean self-esteem score earned by the students at the community school during September, 1990 was 33.2, whereas the value observed during post-testing which occurred during May of 1991 was 34.03.

How teachers interact with their students is most important. Students learn best when they are taught by teachers who establish positive teacher-pupil interactive relationships and provide each of them mutual respect and encouragement.

When teaching self-esteem consider the following seven "secrets" derived from seven principles offered by Berne *(1985)*. She recommends that teachers:

1. **BUILD IN SUCCESS:** To ensure success, teachers should structure tasks into series of easy steps to minimize the probability of failure.

   The self-esteem principle associated with this recommendation is that "Success builds self-esteem, especially when the chain of successes remains continuous and unbroken."

2. **STATE THE POSITIVE:** Teachers should emphasize the positive aspects of their pupils' behavior and transmit information in a nonjudgemental fashion by describing and affirming rather than by judging.

   This follows the principle, "Acknowledging the positive in a non-evaluative but validating way, nurtures success."

3. **CAPITALIZE ON SUCCESSES:** Teachers who capitalize on successes go further than merely capitalizing on interests. Thus, when interests have fostered successes, they go a step further and use these successful experiences to create new successes and expand pupils' interests.

   This is derived from the self-esteem principle that says, "Children will feel success is possible if you can help them build a history of similar successes".

4. **WATCH FOR SPARKS OF GROWTH:** When a child develops a keen interest or spark in a given area provide him or her with encouragement and support. Teachers should use these sparks to assist pupils in developing new skills and learning how to relate to, and interact more effectively with others.

   This comes from the self-esteem principle that holds, "Children with low self-esteem tend to believe they cannot grow, learn, or successfully relate to other people; and often, they won't until a spark of interest is ignited."

5. **VALUE AND ACKNOWLEDGE:** Teachers should acknowledge their students' accomplishments and communicate to them that they value their efforts and contributions.

For Teachers, Parents and Kids:

This is from the principle, "Evidence of success that is visible and tangible has a strong positive effect on a child's self-esteem."

6. KEEP EXPECTATIONS REALISTIC: The expectation that teachers establish for their pupils should be appropriate for their ability, aptitude, and interest. Expectations should be neither too low nor too high, and students need to be treated as partners in the development of skills.

This follows the self-esteem principle, "Clearly stating reasonable expectations will help children with low self-esteem feel less anxious about pleasing others."

7. DON'T BE BORING: Teachers should strive to make their classes and the subject matter they teach as exciting as possible.

This is from the principle, "When children find learning exciting, they tend to learn more effectively."

INTERACTIVE STRATEGIES THAT PARENTS AND TEACHERS CAN USE

The strategies described in this section can be used by both parents and teachers to enhance the self-esteem and achievement levels of children.

There are many programmed packages of activities that authors propose will enhance self-esteem, achievement and development. However, little data is available to support these assumptions. In my view it is not the activity that is most essential for enhancing self-esteem, but rather it is the interactive process that is most crucial. Therefore, in our view activities without effective interactions will not enhance self-esteem and in some instances may, in fact, diminish self-esteem.

Regarding the role that self-esteem plays in the process of development, Dorothy Corkville Briggs in her book entitled *Your Child's Self-Esteem* states:

> True, all children need to experience their competence to build self-respect. But each child needs to feel that his person is cherished regardless of his competence. Successful performances build the sense of worthwhileness; being cherished as a person nurtures the feeling of being loved. Every child needs to feel both loved and worthwhile. But lovability must not be tied to worthwhile performance. The more loveable any child feels, however, the more likely he is to perform in satisfactory ways, for then he likes himself.

Three important groups of caretakers who may function to promote the enhancement of the self-esteem of individuals in our culture are: parents, teachers and psychotherapists. The most important mechanisms that these three individuals employ to enhance the self-esteem of others are interactive strategies.

Interactive strategies that have proven to be effective in enhancing self-esteem and achievement *(Battle, 1982, 1987, 1990, 1993)*, include: a) mutual respect, b) consideration of self-esteem, c) unconditional positive regard, and d) encouragement.

MUTUAL RESPECT
Mutual respect is a cognitive technique in which significant others communicate to an individual that he or she is respected as a unique individual possessing the same basic rights and responsibilities as others of similar age and status.

CONSIDERATION OF SELF-ESTEEM

Teachers should encourage their students to consider the self-esteem of their classmates and others at all times.

When we consider self-esteem we make concerted efforts to ensure that the behavior we display does not exert a negative effect on the self-esteem of the person with whom we are interacting. That is, we do not demean or belittle her. We interact in a fashion in which we at least permit the person to maintain the level of self-esteem that she brings to the interaction. Hopefully, we interact in a fashion in which we enable the student, client or significant other to enhance her self-esteem. Because self-esteem is such an important variable in the lives of humans, its enhancement generally exerts a positive effect on achievement and well being.

UNCONDITIONAL POSITIVE REGARD

Unconditional positive regard, as put forth by Rogers *(1951)*, is a process in which parents communicate to their children that they are loved unconditionally. That is, they communicate to their children that caring for, and prizing them is not contingent on any predetermined conditions. Children who have this from their parents realize that their parents love them at all times, even when they behave in a fashion that their parents consider to be inappropriate.

A question that parents frequently ask is "How can I know if my children feel they are loved unconditionally?" We can never know with absolute certainty how another person perceives the world. If we listen to, and observe our children's behavior closely, however, we can make reliable inferences regarding how they view themselves and others.

Two examples are provided as illustrations of how we can determine if our children perceive that they are loved unconditionally.

Because my wife Dorothy and I feel that communication of unconditional positive regard is so critical, we made concerted efforts to make it as clear as possible to our children at a very early stage in their development that our love for them was without conditions, provided freely, simply because they were our children. For instance, when our daughter Christina was between the ages of two and a half and five, whenever I disciplined her (e.g., I rapped her on the hands approximately four times during this period), I would tell her that I loved her but that I was "spanking" her because I felt her behavior required that form of intervention. When our son, Jamie was the same age, I rapped his hands perhaps eight to 10 times; and when I applied this form of discipline to Jamie, Christina would put her arms around him and say, "Now, Jamie, he loves you; he just didn't like what you did." The observation led me to conclude that Christina knows she is loved unconditionally. When I tuck Jamie into bed at night, I kiss him and say, "Good night son; your Dad loves you". His reply is always "I know; I love you too Dad". That leads me to conclude that Jamie knows he is loved unconditionally.

ENCOURAGEMENT

I recommend that parents consistently encourage their children as they interact with them. Parents who encourage their children emphasize positives rather than negatives. They minimize the importance of children's mistakes while recognizing and helping to build their assets and strengths.

For Teachers, Parents and Kids:

TEACHER STRATEGIES THAT PROMOTE SELF-ESTEEM AND ACHIEVEMENT

To assist children in functioning more effectively academically, which should in turn exert a positive effect on their self-esteem, teachers should teach them strategies that will enable them to perform "smarter" rather than "harder" as many individuals advocate. The following are recommended strategies for teachers to use when instructing students in a) reading, b) spelling, c) arithmetic, and d) visual imagery.

READING

1. Teachers should provide the child with reading tasks that are short and fairly simple initially and increase the complexity of the tasks gradually.

2. Teachers should use a systematic, structured approach to reading that emphasizes both visual and auditory modalities.

3. Teachers should use a revisualization process to teach sight words.

The recommended sequence is:

   a. Have the child look at a flashcard with a new sight word printed on it, and have the child repeat the word after it is pronounced to him.

   b. Have the child trace the word in the air, using his entire, extended arm, pointing and tracing with the pointer and index fingers. If the child forms any of the letters of the word incorrectly, have him repeat the process while spelling the word orally.

c. Have the child close his eyes and try to revisualize the sequence of letters that make the word. Then, tell him to trace the word from memory, spelling it aloud simultaneously with his eyes closed, trying to see a picture of the letters while he is performing this task.

d. Have the child test himself by writing the word from memory. If he cannot write the word from memory, show him the word again, and repeat the earlier steps (a, b, and c). Remind the child to spell the word subvocally ("under his breath"), as he writes and repeats the word before he writes it and again after he writes it.

e. Give the child a group of flashcards that include the word being taught and other words of similar configuration - for example, friend, frend, freind, frand....

4. Teachers should encourage the child to read to the class, starting with short and fairly simple material initially, and increasing the length and complexity of the material gradually to ensure success and minimize the probability of failure.

5. In their reading program, teachers should also teach students to write in context.

Recommended steps to writing in context are:

1. COPY - Children copy from the chalkboard a content-vocabulary word that the teacher knows they will encounter as they read.

For Teachers, Parents and Kids:

2. **GUESS MEANING** - Children read the text silently until they encounter the copied word. At this point they stop and try to write down a synonym or short definition. Guessing is encouraged, as is quick response time.

3. **RE-READ** - The teacher re-reads aloud to the children the paragraph containing the word, carefully noting context clues, margin notes, or any graphic aids to meaning that can be used to figure out the word.

4. **REVISE** - Children are then asked to use the new information to revise the original meaning they wrote *(Glazer & Searfoss, 1988, pp. 220).*

SPELLING

1. Teachers should expose their children to spelling words that are fairly simple (e.g. one syllable), initially and increase the length and complexity of the words gradually.

2. Teachers should use the Fitzgerald Method to teach children to spell. When using the Fitzgerald Method, the recommended sequence is:

   a. Have the student look at the word.

   b. Have the student pronounce the word.

   c. Have the student pronounce the word again with eyes closed.

   d. Cover up the word and have the student write it.

   e. If the word is spelled incorrectly, begin the sequence again.

3. Teachers should use a neurolinguistic approach to teach spelling. When using a neurolinguistic approach, the recommended sequence is:

    a. Write down the word the student is to spell on a card.

    b. Show the card to the student.

    c. Remove the card from the student's view.

    d. Teach the student to use visual imagery or construct pictures of the word to be spelled.

    e. Have the child spell the word forward.

    f. Then, have the child spell the word backwards.

ARITHMETIC

1. Teachers should provide students with simple arithmetic tasks at first, and gradually increase complexity.

2. Teachers should teach students how to use internal dialogue to solve arithmetic tasks.

3. Teachers should use a visual imagery sequence to teach multiplication facts.

4. Teachers should present arithmetic tasks in a sequence which permits the child to perform all of the complementary operations and at the same time learn basic facts.

The recommended sequence is illustrated by the following:

$$\begin{array}{cc} 9 \\ \underline{\times\,3} \\ 27 \end{array} \quad \begin{array}{cc} 3 \\ \underline{\times\,9} \\ 27 \end{array} \quad 3\overline{)27} \quad 9\overline{)27} \quad 3\times9=27 \quad 9\times3=27$$

       For Teachers, Parents and Kids:

5. Teachers may use long but simple problems to help students "overlearn" operations and facts.

888	321, 742, 134, 521	892, 678, 542
- 333	+134, 151, 341, 237	-151, 265, 321

VISUAL IMAGERY

To facilitate the development of visual imagery skills, teachers should:

1. Have a student read a text and make a drawing of what he/she read. A second student reads the text and reacts to the first student's drawing. After discussion, they develop a new drawing.

2. Have all students draw pictures from a text they read, and compare their drawings and reactions.

3. Have students write a text, after seeing a picture, that changes the still picture into a dynamic episode. Share the texts and have students decide which text most accurately represents the picture.

4. Help students to induce a particular mental image. Then read a text to them. After reading, ask them in what ways they had to modify their image in order to accommodate the text. Ask if imagery helps them to recall.

5. Use pictures when reading a book to children. Try sharing the pictures before, during and after reading.

6. Use facsimile artifacts related to a character in evoking images in children. These aid in building a background of knowledge for reading.

7. Allow students to see movies or filmstrips of stories prior to reading them. After the reading, discuss which version was preferred.

8. Use visual image activities as enjoyable culminating events to stories that are read; use pictures or cartoons to dramatize certain events from the story.

9. Extend a completed story by having students draw an 8 or 12 frame cartoon of a succeeding chapter.

10. Describe an ordinary item, orally, or in writing, by its elements. Have students draw a representation of the object from the verbal description; compare drawings.

11. Show the students only a portion of a picture. Ask them to verbalize, using oral or written language to describe the entire picture.

12. Have students hypothesize an upcoming chapter or episode in a book, by drawing a cartoon of their predictions. Follow up with evaluations of their predictions.

When providing imagery-building activities, teachers should ensure that the activities offered combine sign and symbol. Thus, imagery activities should connect language to images, and images to language *(Battle, 1990, pp. 23-76).*

PARENT STRATEGIES THAT PROMOTE SELF-ESTEEM AND ACHIEVEMENT

In order for parents to model behavior which promote the development of positive self-esteem and achievement in their children, they must possess positive perceptions of

For Teachers, Parents and Kids:

their own worth so that they can communicate this disposition to the children *(James Battle, 1988; 1990).*

Parents should provide their children:

1. **APPROPRIATE STIMULATION** - Children who are exposed to insufficient environmental stimulation will be handicapped in their ability to adjust. Children should be provided appropriate (i.e., neither insufficient nor excessive), stimulation, with the amount of stimulation being geared to the child's needs.

2. **DEMOCRATIC CHILD-REARING** - In a democratic home environment the child is able to express his or her views and feelings without fear of rejection or reprimand.

3. **STRAIGHT COMMUNICATIONS** - Communications between parent and child should be clear and straight forward. Thus, communication should not mask or deceive intentions or be double-binded (i.e., dual messages that contradict each other).

4. **MUTUAL RESPECT** - Parents who provide their children mutual respect communicate to them that they have basic rights.

5. **UNCONDITIONAL POSITIVE REGARD** - Parents who provide their children unconditional positive regard communicate to them that their loving them is not contingent on any predetermined conditions. That is, loving them is provided freely and is not determined by the behavior they display.

6. **ENCOURAGEMENT** - Parents who encourage their children emphasize their assets and strengths,

rather than negatives. Thus, they emphasize positive aspects of their children's behavior rather than negative aspects.

7. **OPPORTUNITIES FOR SUCCESS** - Parents should provide ample opportunities for their children to experience success. Parents should expose their children to tasks that are fairly simple initially and increase the complexity of the tasks gradually to ensure success and minimize the possibility of failure.

8. **OPENNESS IN EXPRESSING FEELINGS** - Parents should encourage their children to recognize feelings (both positive and negative), and deal with them directly, rather than disguise or avoid them.

9. **CONSISTENCY AND FLEXIBILITY** - Parents should be consistent and at the same time open to new ideas and innovative approaches in their interactions with their children.

TEACHERS ENCOURAGING TEACHERS

Self-esteem is an important variable affecting the lives of all humans *(Battle, 1982, 1987)*. Thus the need for positive self-esteem in teachers is as crucial as it is for other groups. Also, because teachers play a major role in the development of children in our culture, it is important that they possess positive self-esteem. Teachers with high self-esteem generally exert a positive effect on their students self-esteem and development, whereas the converse occurs when teachers possess low self-esteem. The need to attend to teachers' self-esteem was addressed by Thomas *(1980)*, when he stated, "Teachers, not only pupils must recognize the need to improve their own behavior, to maintain their

For Teachers, Parents and Kids:

mental health, to get satisfaction through self-sufficiency, to be emotionally mature and to learn to benefit from personal mistakes and successes." *(pp. 39)*

The demands placed on teachers who provide instruction for students in our rapidly changing contemporary society have created a high degree of stress which heavily taxes the coping mechanisms of this group of professionals. Data derived from research findings which indicate that a significant proportion of teachers received disability benefits *(e.g. Jevne and Zingle, 1992)* provides support for this position. Because of this, I am of the opinion that it is important for teachers to provide support and encouragement for each other. The following are some strategies that teachers can use to encourage one another which should, in turn, assist them in their attempts to promote the self-esteem, achievement and behavioral self-control of their students:

1. Each month write a brief letter to a colleague thanking her for her contributions, cooperation and support.

2. Give colleagues cards with encouraging statements when recognizing their birthdays or other occasions.

3. Each morning greet colleagues with positive statements.

4. End conversations with colleagues with positive statements such as "have a good day".

5. Purchase surprise gifts for colleagues.

6. Offer to assist colleagues in areas that are important to them. These may include:

- researching and writing papers.
- purchasing a car.
- acquiring a mortgage for a home.
- dealing with their children.
- dealing with marital conflict.

SUMMARY

1. Self-Esteem is a growth-oriented process which is strongly affected by perception.

2. Perception influences behavior.

3. Teachers can augment the self-esteem and achievement patterns of their pupils.

4. How teachers interact with their pupils affects students' perceptions of self-worth.

5. Teachers should function as advocates of their pupils.

6. Teachers should enhance the self-esteem of their students because self-esteem is highly associated with achievement.

7. Self-esteem is a better predictor of academic success than measured intelligence.

8. Parents can augment the self-esteem and achievement patterns of their children.

9. Parents exert the strongest effect on the self-esteem of their children.

10. Parents should provide clearly defined limits regarding their children's behavior.

For Teachers, Parents and Kids:

11. Parents should make it clear to their children that their loving and caring for them is unconditional.

12. Children should be required to deal with the consequences of their actions.

13. Teachers are basically responsible for the learning of students in the elementary, junior high and senior high years.

14. The interactive process is most important in enhancing the self-esteem of students.

15. Students learn best when they are taught by teachers who establish positive teacher-pupil interactive relationships and provide each of them mutual respect and encouragement.

16. Teachers should encourage their students to consider the self-esteem of their classmates and others at all times.

17. Teachers and parents should teach children to perform smarter.

18. Teachers should encourage each other.

CHAPTER 3

Promoting Self-Esteem and Behavioral Self-Control

THERE IS A CRUCIAL NEED to promote self-esteem and behavioral self-control among students because incidents of violence continue to escalate in our schools and communities. Because of this, it is important that our children and youth be taught behavioral self-control. Behavioral self-control refers to the process in which an individual deliberately alters or changes his or her behavior to achieve a specific goal. Karen Esveldt-Dawson and Alan E. Kazdin *(1983)*, Coopersmith *(1967)* commented that "Probably the most important requirement for effective behavior control to the whole problem is self-esteem." Two important contemporary behavior problems associated with children and youth that requires the promotion of self-control are Attention Deficit Hyperactivity Disorder and Conduct Disorder.

ATTENTION-DEFICIT HYPERACTIVITY DISORDER

Attention Deficit Hyperactivity Disorder is a common behavior problem that affects individuals of all socio-economic groups and cultures. For instance, in the United States, Great Britain, Australia, Germany and China, approximately two to three percent of girls and six to nine percent of boys are diagnosed as being hyperactive. *(Battle, 1990, p.76)*. Also, data derived from follow-up studies of clinic samples indicate that approximately one-third of children with ADHD continue to show signs of the disorder in adulthood *(DSM III-R, 1987, p. 51)*.

The list of notable persons who were hyperactive children is long and includes individuals such as Thomas Edison and Winston Churchill. Thomas Edison was so hyperactive his mother withdrew him from school and taught him herself. Winston Churchill's first governess resigned because she considered him to be an extremely disruptible incorrigible child. Churchill was so hyperactive his teacher at one school permitted him to leave the classroom at regular intervals and run around the school grounds in order to "wear off" some energy.

Attention-Deficit Hyperactivity Disorder is a condition which is characterized by developmentally inappropriate degrees of inattention, impulsiveness and hyperactivity. The child with ADHD often fidgets with hands or feet, is easily distractible and almost always experience difficulties sustaining attention.

CONDUCT DISORDERS

Conduct Disorders are characterized by behavior that is unacceptable to others. The essential feature of this disorder is a persistent pattern of conduct in which the basic rights of others and major age-appropriate societal norms or rules are violated *(DSM-III-R, APA, 1987)*.

Conduct Disorders are commonly identified problems of children and youth. For instance, relevant data reported in the literature indicate that one-third to one-half of all children referred to Child Guidance and other mental health clinics are referred for problems associated with conduct. *(Roach 1958; Wiltz and Pattern, 1974; Wolff, 1961).*

For Teachers, Parents and Kids:

Common characteristics of children experiencing Conduct Disorders includes: stealing, lying, running away from home, fighting and destruction of others' property.

PROMOTING SELF-ESTEEM AND BEHAVIORAL SELF-CONTROL OF CHILDREN WITH ADHD: STRATEGIES FOR TEACHERS

The strategies recommended in Chapter 2 (e.g. mutual respect; consideration of self-esteem; encouragement) can be used by teachers to promote the self-esteem and behavioral self-control of students who are experiencing Attention Deficit Hyperactivity Disorders. In addition, the following are recommended:

1. Provide clear and concise instructions.

2. Provide rewards when the child displays effort and improvement.

3. Provide instructions in short, systematic sequences.

4. Make an "extra' effort to ensure that the pupil understands instructions prior to commencing task.

5. Teach the student to "self-correct" when performing academic tasks.

6. Keep routines consistent and predictable.

7. Provide the pupil alternatives to deal with difficult situations, (e.g., there will be a lot of noise and distractions in class today, make sure that you try real hard to concentrate and listen; there will be lots of people in the gym today making lots of noise, you will have to listen and concentrate really hard in order to get the instructions from your coach).

8. Permit the student to work for brief periods of time with intermittent "breaks" for relaxation.

9. Provide the student short, untimed assignments.

10. When required provide the student earphones that eliminate extraneous stimuli.

11. Provide the student short assignments initially, and increase the complexity of tasks gradually to ensure success and minimize the probability of failure.

12. If necessary use study carrels or cubicles to facilitate concentration and minimize distractibility.

13. Meet the student in the corridor prior to him entering his class in the morning and afternoons, and remind him to try his best to stay in his seat, concentrate on what the teacher says and focus his attention. For example, "remember Bill to try your best to listen to instructions, stay in your desk and concentrate on your work".

14. At the end of the school day reward the student for effort and improvement.

15. Remind the pupil to do her best to stay in her seat until she is given permission to leave, complete assignments, and interact cooperatively with peers and staff.

16. Teach the student to use visual-imagery to facilitate impulse control and ability to sustain attention.

17. Use a stop watch to establish the time it takes the student to get organized, commence tasks and complete assignments.

For Teachers, Parents and Kids:

Promoting Self-Esteem and Behavioral Self-Control of Children with ADHD: Strategies for Parents

The following are some strategies that parents can use to promote the self-esteem and behavioral self-control of the child who is experiencing Attention Deficit Hyperactivity Disorders:

1. Emphasize positive rather than negative aspects of your child's behavior.

2. Reward your child when she behaves appropriately and withhold the rewards when she misbehaves.

3. Teach your child to use self-talk to facilitate his ability to focus attention. For example, teaching him to rehearse verbal statements (e.g. to tell himself to slow down; listen really hard), designed to assist him in maintaining attention more effectively.

4. Teach your child to monitor her own behavior and keep track of the length of time she stays on task and focuses her attention appropriately.

5. Teach your child to reward him or her self for focussing appropriately (e.g., I did great; I'm getting better).

PROMOTING SELF-ESTEEM AND BEHAVIORAL SELF-CONTROL OF CHILDREN WITH CONDUCT DISORDERS: STRATEGIES FOR TEACHERS

The strategies recommended in Chapter 2 (e.g., mutual respect; encouragement, consideration of self-esteem) can be used by teachers to promote the self-esteem and behavioral self-control of their students who are experiencing conduct disorders. In addition, the following strategies are recommended:

1. Provide the child with a structured classroom environment with clearly defined limits that are enforced consistently.

2. Clarify expectations for the child and require him to deal with the consequences of his actions.

3. Emphasize positive rather than negative aspects of the child's behavior and reprimand only when absolutely necessary. In those few instances, reprimand as privately and quietly as possible.

4. Permit the child to work in an environment that has little stimulation (e.g., a cubicle), when behavior is disruptive enough to impede the progress of other students.

5. Allow the child to take "time out" or remove himself from the classroom when he becomes frustrated or when behavior is disruptive.

6. Expose the child to reinforcement contingencies designed to promote desirable behavior and extinguish undesirable behavior.

For Teachers, Parents and Kids:

7. Provide the child support, encourage him to manage his behavior more effectively, and permit him to deal with the consequences of his actions.

8. Offer legitimate rewards for appropriate behavior.

9. Provide a highly structured, comprehensive program that attends to cognitive (academic), affective (emotional) and conduct (behavioral) needs.

Promoting Self-Esteem and Behavioral Self-Control of Children with Conduct Disorders: Strategies for Parents

The Strategies recommended in Chapter 2 (e.g., mutual respect; consideration for self-esteem; encouragement) can be used by parents to promote the self-esteem and behavioral self-control of their children who are experiencing conduct disorders. In addition to these, the following strategies are recommended:

1. Emphasize the positive aspects of your child's behavior, not negative ones.

2. Encourage your child to manage her behavior more appropriately and permit her to deal with the consequences of her behavior.

3. Assist your child in clarifying his expectations and permit him to deal with the consequences of his actions.

4. Provide your child reinforcement contingencies designed to promote desirable behavior and extinguish undesirable behavior.

5. Assist your child in choosing modes of behavior that are self-enhancing rather than self-defeating.

6. Show your child how to explore alternatives.

7. Teach your child how to assess the probable consequences of alternatives.

8. Provide your child clearly defined limits that are enforced consistently.

9. Facilitate the development of "appropriate" behavior in your child by offering rewards (e.g., permission to participate in preferred self-selected activities, giving attention) when behavior meets expectations.

PROMOTING THE SELF-ESTEEM AND BEHAVIORAL SELF-CONTROL OF REGULAR CHILDREN AND STUDENTS: STRATEGIES FOR TEACHERS

The strategies recommended in Chapter 2 (e.g. mutual respect; consideration of self-esteem; encouragement) and those listed earlier in this chapter for helping children experiencing ADHD and Conduct Disorders can be used by teachers to assist regular children and students. In addition, teachers in their attempts to promote behavioral self-control and the self-esteem of their pupils should establish a positive teacher-pupil interactive process with their students.

A positive teacher-pupil interactive process is one in which the teacher lets the pupil know that:

For Teachers, Parents and Kids:

"He is an individual who is worthy and significant... and that this evaluation is not contingent on any pre-determined conditions. It is a process in which the teacher provides structure for the child . . . and communicates to him that he is expected to perform and behave in a certain fashion. It is also communicated to the child that he can determine whether or not he will function in the expected fashion . . . and that he will have to assume the responsibility for his actions".
(Battle, 1982, pp.23-24).

Teachers can establish this supportive, well-structured environment. Although teachers will obviously use different approaches in their attempts to establish positive teacher-pupil interactions, the strategies delineated in the following pages are intended to serve as models which may be used by elementary, junior high and high school teachers. These examples focus on the teacher's introduction on the first day of a new class, since "first impressions" set the tone for how the entire school term will progress.

ELEMENTARY LEVEL STRATEGIES

On the first day of class, the elementary school teacher might say something like this:

'Welcome, boys and girls to grade . . . I am your teacher, Mrs. Jones. I would like each of you to know that I am very pleased and excited to have this opportunity to work with you this year. However, before we begin our work, I would like to have a brief discussion with you. I would like to start our discussion by sharing with you some of my feelings.

First, I would like you to know that I care for and respect each one of you. Also my caring for, and respecting you is not due to any special reasons. I feel that each of you is important, and that teachers and students do the best schoolwork when they care for and respect each other. So, remember that I will always care for and respect you, even when there are problems. For instance, sometimes during the year, I will insist that some of you do certain things — maybe even things that you may not want to do. I will make you do these things because I feel they are best for you. I will, however, care for and respect you at all times — when things are going well and even when things are not going well.

Second, I have expectations for each of you. For instance, I expect each of you to do your schoolwork and behave appropriately. Third, I would like to meet each of you. So, when I call your name, please raise your hand.

After the teacher calls the roll and recognizes each student, she might say, "Are there any questions or comments?" After the teacher entertains all questions and comments, regularly scheduled tasks may commence.

JUNIOR HIGH LEVEL STRATEGIES

On the first day of class, the junior high school teacher might say:

'Welcome to grade . . . I am Mr. Wilson, the homeroom teacher for section . . . . During this first class, I would like to do two things. First, I would like to meet each of you; and second, I would like to conduct a brief class discussion'. [The teacher calls the roll, acknowledging each student individually.]

For Teachers, Parents and Kids:

'I would like to start our discussion by sharing with you some of my feelings. The first — and probably the most important — thing I would like to say is that I care for you and respect each of you individually. Also, I would like for each of you to know that my caring for and respecting you is not due to or dependent on, any special conditions. I care for and respect you because you are who you are: simply because you are my pupils'.

'I would also like to say that I have expectations for you. For instance, I expect each of you to do your best school work, attend classes regularly, and behave appropriately. I realize that each of you will have to decide whether or not you will behave in the expected fashion; however, the decision about that is one that you must make. Only you can make this decision; and, of course, each of you will have to take responsibility for your decisions and behavior. I hope each of you will make decisions that will be the best ones for you. I will, of course, care for you and respect you at all times — even when there are problems — because I feel that this is the best way for teachers and students to get along together. I feel that, if we care for and respect each other, it will be best for all of us — best for you and best for me'.

After the teacher finishes stating personal feelings and views, he should ask if there are any questions or comments. After he entertains all questions and comments, he may begin regularly scheduled tasks.

High School Level Strategies

On the first day, the high school teacher should begin by ensuring that pupils are in the right classroom. Immediately afterward, he might say:

'I am Mr. Robinson, the homeroom teacher for grade . . . , section . . . . The first thing I would like to do today is to meet each of you individually. I am going to call the roll; when I call your name, hold up your hand; and, if you like, you may make a brief statement regarding your interests and what you want to accomplish this year. If you don't have any comments to make, however, please do not feel compelled to do so.' [The teacher calls the roll and listens to students tell about their interests].

'There are two additional things I would like to do during this period. First, I would like to share with you some of my interests; and second, I would like to share some of my feelings with you'. [The teacher spends a few minutes talking about personal academic interests.]

'At this point, I'd like to share some of my feelings. I am of the opinion that students and teachers function best when they care for and respect each other. I believe this, and so I care for and respect each of you individually. Moreover, my caring for and respecting you is unconditional and will be maintained at all times — when things are going well and even when we have difficulties'.

'I would also like to say that each of you will be expected to perform and behave in a given fashion, — a fashion determined by school administrative personnel and me. Each of you, however, will have to determine whether or not you will perform according to these expectations; and, of course, each of you will have to assume responsibility for your actions'.

For Teachers, Parents and Kids:

After the teacher has expressed his feelings and views, he should ask for questions and comments from class members. Following the discussion, regularly scheduled tasks may begin.

Teachers should also utilize "positives" to promote self-esteem and assist the child in managing his or her behavior more appropriately. In order to accomplish this result, when the child emits "appropriate" behavior, use statements that:

1. **DEMONSTRATE ACCEPTANCE** - for example:
   a) I'm pleased that you are sitting at your desk and getting your work done.
   b) I'm pleased that you are listening to me and doing what I tell you to do.
   c) I'm pleased to see that you are getting along with the other children.
   d) I'm pleased to see that you are listening to and helping others.
   e) I'm glad that you like being in my class because I sure like being your teacher.

2. **RECOGNIZE CONTRIBUTIONS** - for example:
   a) Thanks for helping me with . . . ; it makes my job so much easier.
   b) Thanks for cooperating with your classmates today; I surely appreciate it.
   c) Thanks for cooperating with me today; I appreciate it.

3. **RECOGNIZE EFFORT AND IMPROVEMENT** - for example:
   a) You worked... all ... most ... part of the day; I thank you very much.
   b) Thanks for getting your work out when I told you to.

c) Thanks for coming in right after recess, I appreciate it.

d) You worked all day and I didn't have to remind you, thanks very much.

It is also important that teachers set expectations for their students, because when they establish expectations, it increases the probability of achieving desired results. Also, when teachers set expectations, the result is usually a self-fulfilling prophecy, characterized by a tendency to behave in a fashion that is in concert with previously established expectations.

The expectations that teachers set for their students should be realistic and obtainable. However, if one must error, she should error on the high side, because if she set expectations too low, she generally limits the students progress. This occurs because once expectations are set, both the child and the teacher tends to behave in a fashion to ensure that prophecies are fulfilled. Research findings support this position and indicate that teachers who set high expectations for their students obtain higher levels of academic performance from them than teachers who set low expectations. As stated earlier, the expectations teachers possess regarding what they feel students can and cannot learn often become self-fulfilling prophecies. Because of this, students tend to learn as little or as much as their teachers expect. Also, when teachers expect less from students, they tend to treat them differently and usually:

- give them less direct instruction
- have them sit farther away from the teacher's desk
- ask them to do less work
- provide them fewer opportunities to learn new material

- call on them less frequently and when they do, the questions they ask are generally simple, basic non-complex ones
- provide them less time to respond to questions and give them less help when their answers are incorrect

The perception and expectation that an individual, in a position of power possesses regarding an individual's behavior can lead to a self-fulfilling prophecy; in which the victim emits behavior, which ensures that the expectation is realized. For example, if a football coach possesses the perception that his field goal kicker is a poor kicker and the expectation that he cannot kick field goals consistently, the kicker will generally tend to kick in a fashion (emit behavior) to ensure that the expectation of his coach is realized (self-fulfilling prophecy).

If a teacher possesses the perception and expectation that a given student is a poor reader, the student will tend to ensure that this prophecy is fulfilled. For example, a colleague asked me to recommend a school for his son that was near the university he taught at. Shortly after he enrolled his son in the school that I recommended, the boy's teacher asked my friend to come to the school for a parent-teacher interview to discuss his son's reading difficulties. During the interview the teacher told my friend that his son had a reading problem and recommended that he be placed in a resource room. (A small group classroom for students experiencing learning problems.) During the interview a teacher on the staff of the school, who was taking a course from my friend at the university, came in the staff room where they were meeting, recognized him and said, "Hi Dr. —, How are you?" After this, the interviewing teacher made a dramatic change in the statements she was making regarding his son's ability. She had incorporated the perception and expectation that his son was not a capable student and would not do well in reading. His son, however, was reading at a grade three level when he was in grade one, and his year one teacher had recommended that he be accelerated.

PROMOTING THE SELF-ESTEEM AND BEHAVIORAL SELF-CONTROL OF REGULAR CHILDREN AND STUDENTS: STRATEGIES FOR PARENTS

The Strategies recommended in chapter 2 (e.g., mutual respect; consideration of self-esteem; encouragement) and those listed earlier in this chapter for helping children experiencing ADHD and Conduct Disorders can be used by parents to assist regular children and students. In addition, the following are recommended:

1. Provide your child structure and limits that are enforced consistently.

2. Permit your child to express his or her views without fear of rejection or reprimand. However, if you disagree with your child's views, make it clear to him and require him to do certain things that you consider to be best for him.

3. Establish expectations for your child. It is essential for you to set expectations for children because when you establish expectations, it increases the probability of achieving desired results. Also, when expectations are set, the result is usually a self-fulfilling prophecy, characterized by a tendency to behave in a fashion that is in concert with previously established

For Teachers, Parents and Kids:

expectations. The expectations for your children should be realistic and obtainable. However, if one must error, he should error on the high side, because if he set expectations that are too low he generally limits their progress. This occurs because once expectations are set both the child and parent tends to behave in a fashion to ensure that prophecies are fulfilled.

BEHAVIORAL SELF-CONTROL

Gage (1965) states:

"The ultimate goal of all education is to wean students progressively from dependence upon teachers, and teach them to do what is necessary to guide their own behavior."

I am of the opinion that it is important that teachers, parents and other providers of care promote the development of behavioral self-control in children and youth. With age-appropriate behavioral self-control children can deliberately alter or change their behavior to achieve desired goals. Some strategies that promote behavioral self-control are: self-assessment, self-monitoring and self-reinforcement.

SELF-ASSESSMENT

When an individual employs the strategy of self-assessment he systematically examines his own behavior in order to determine whether or not he has performed a specific behavior or group of behaviors.

The most commonly used type of self-assessment is self-rating. When teaching self-rating have each of your students make a scale like the one presented in Figure 2:1 to rate his or her behavior.

Figure 2:1. Behavior Self-Rating Form

Directions: Please rate yourself in the following fashion for each period. If you meet your expectations give yourself a check (✓) in the appropriate space. If you do not meet expectations withhold the check.

PERIOD		ARRIVE ON TIME	STRIVING TO SUCCEED	COMPLETION OF ASSIGNMENTS	APPROPRIATE BEHAVIOR	CHECK
MON	8:30 - 10:15					
	10:30 - 12:00					
	12:30 - 2:30					
	2:45 - 4:30					
TUE	8:30 - 10:15					
	10:30 - 12:00					
	12:30 - 2:30					
	2:45 - 4:30					
WED	8:30 - 10:15					
	10:30 - 12:00					
	12:30 - 2:30					
	2:45 - 4:30					
THUR	8:30 - 10:15					
	10:30 - 12:00					
	12:30 - 2:30					
	2:45 - 4:30					
FRI	8:30 - 10:15					
	10:30 - 12:00					
	12:30 - 2:30					
	2:45 - 4:30					
TOTAL:						

Signature Teacher: _____

Signature Student: _____

For Teachers, Parents and Kids:

Principals, teachers, parents and kids can use the *Special Assignment Form and Daily Self-Assessment Form* presented in Figures 2.2 and 2.3 to promote behavioral self-control and display of "appropriate" behavior.

FIGURE 2:2. SPECIAL ASSIGNMENT FORM

DIRECTIONS: You are to do the following assignment and return it to the Principal for approval upon your return to school. Your teacher is expected to read it and discuss it with you. Please have your teacher sign it at the bottom of your work to indicate that it has been discussed.

TOPIC TO BE ADDRESSED: _____

_____

DATE DUE: _____

ASSIGNED TO STUDENT: _____

MY SIDE OF THE STORY

1. Write a paragraph of no less than _____ words explaining what happened. Make sure it includes what, who, why, when and where.

2. Write a second paragraph of no less than _____ words about whether this should be a concern of _____ School. Make sure it includes all possible reasons why or why not.

3. Write a third paragraph of no less than _____ words about what should be done to prevent, change, or correct this behavior or incident from happening again.

4. Write a fourth paragraph of no less than _____ words sharing what you have learned by doing this exercise.

SOURCE: *Tkachuk, Ron. Edmonton Public Schools, Edmonton, Alberta. Reproduced by permission of the author.*

FIGURE 2:3. DAILY ASSESSMENT FORM

DIRECTIONS: This report is a record of how the undersigned student saw his behavior during the date indicated, compared to his teacher's perception. It is to be completed daily by the student without any reminders. It is to be taken home at the end of the day after a brief meeting with the teacher and returned to the principal in the morning after being reviewed by the parents. Points are to be awarded as per the following:

    0 need for improvement
    1 some effort made
    2 good effort made
    3 super effort made

	STUDENT'S SELF-ASSESSMENT	TEACHER'S ASSESSMENT
I came to class on time, prepared to work.		
While in class I remained on task and completed my assignments neatly.		
During the day I demonstrated respect for fellow students, adults, property and rules.		
I made special extra efforts today to demonstrate responsibility, without suggestion by any other person.		
TOTAL		
DATE:	STUDENT:	
STUDENT'S SIGNATURE		
TEACHER'S COMMENT		
TEACHER'S SIGNATURE		
PARENT'S COMMENT		
PARENT'S SIGNATURE		
A completed report is to be handed in to the principal each day, at which time a new form will be picked up and shown to the classroom teacher for admission to class.		
DATE REVIEWED	PRINCIPAL'S SIGNATURE	

SOURCE: Tkachuk, Ron. Edmonton Public Schools, Edmonton, Alberta..
Reproduced by permission of the author.

SELF-MONITORING

Self-Monitoring is a procedure in which the individual systematically monitors and records her performance of certain behaviors, and keeps a record of how often and to what extent she engages in some activity.

The most commonly used type of self-monitoring is Frequency Self-Monitoring. Frequency Self-Monitoring is a procedure in which an individual monitors and records the number of times a given behavior occurs. When teaching Frequency Self-Monitoring have each student make a scale like the one in Figure 2.4 to monitor his or her behavior.

FIGURE 2:4. FREQUENCY SELF-MONITORING SCALE

DIRECTIONS: For each day, place a check (✓) each time I give you/the class an instruction and you follow it immediately.

MONDAY	
TUESDAY	
WEDNESDAY	
THURSDAY	
FRIDAY	

NAME: _____

WEEK: _____

SELF-REINFORCEMENT

Self-Reinforcement is a procedure in which individuals give themselves reinforcers when they display behavior that is "appropriate". The two most commonly employed types of self-reinforcement are:

OVERT SELF-REINFORCEMENT -A procedure in which individuals administer overt (observable and tangible) reinforcers to themselves after they engage in certain appropriate behaviors.

COVERT POSITIVE REINFORCEMENT - A procedure in which individuals are taught to administer non-tangible (e.g. to visualize being on task and to imagine receiving a highly valued reward for being on task) reinforcers to themselves for appropriate behaviors.

SOURCE: Edward A. Workman. Teaching Behavioral Self-Control to Students. 1982, Pro-Ed.

I also recommend that teachers, parents and other providers of care use Behavior Monitoring Schedules such as those illustrated in Figures 2:5, 2:6, 2:7 and 2:8 in their attempts to promote behavioral self-control in the children and students they serve.

FIGURE 2:5. BEHAVIOR MONITORING SCHEDULE

DIRECTIONS: Please rate Tony in the following fashion for each period. If he meets the expectations, give him a check (✓) in the appropriate space. If he does not meet expectations, withhold the check.

PERIOD	COMPLETION OF CLASS ASSIGNMENTS	BEHAVIOR DISTRACTION OF PEERS	ATTENTION (ON TASK) FOCUSING	S.O.T. START ON TIME
8:40 - 9:00				
9:00 - 9:50				
RECESS				
10:30 - 11:00				
11:00 - 11:30				
11:30 - 11:50				
LUNCH				
1:10 - 1:30				
1:30 - 1:45				
1:45 - 2:15				
RECESS				
2:30 - 3:00				
3:00 - 3:30				

Signature
Student: _____

Signature
Teacher:_____

Signature
Parent: _____

Signature
Principal: _____

RATING SCHEDULE: Classroom performance maximum = 48 checks
Playground/behavior = 2checks

FIGURE 2:6. BEHAVIOR MONITORING SCHEDULE

DIRECTIONS: Please rate the student as follows for each period. If the student meets the expectations rate him or her with a " □ ". If he or she does not meet the expectations rate him or her with a " ○ ".

Variable	Date	Period 1		Period 2		Period 3		Period 4	
		am	pm	am	pm	am	pm	am	pm
Organizational Skills									
Study Habits									
Impulse Control									
Time on Task									

Signature Student: _____

Signature Teacher: _____

Signature Parent: _____

Signature Principal: _____

(Battle, 1990)

FIGURE 2:7. BEHAVIOR MONITORING SCHEDULE

DIRECTIONS: Please rate the student each period daily. The rating range is from 1 (poor) to 5 (excellent). Assign one rating each period per day and make your comments in the evaluation column.

Period	Date	Evaluation	1 2 3 4 5	Homework	Behavior
1					
2					
3					
4					
5					
6					
7					

Signature Student: _____

Signature Teacher: _____

Signature Parent: _____

Signature Principal: _____

For Teachers, Parents and Kids:

FIGURE 2:8. BEHAVIOR MONITORING SCHEDULE

DIRECTIONS: Please rate your child as follows for each day. If your child meets the expectations rate him or her with a " □ ". If your child does not meet the expectations rate him or her with a " ○ ".

Variable															
Sunday pm															
Sunday am															
Saturday pm															
Saturday am															
Friday pm															
Friday am															
Thursday pm															
Thursday am															
Wednesday pm															
Wednesday am															
Tuesday pm															
Tuesday am															
Monday pm															
Monday am															

Signature Parent: _____

Signature Child: _____

PROBLEM RESOLUTION STRATEGIES

Teachers, parents and other care providers can use a variety of problem resolution strategies in their attempts to promote the self-esteem and behavioral self-control of the children they serve. The ones that I have found to be effective are: a) The A-B-C Paradigm b) Reflective Listening and c) The Jig-Saw Puzzle technique.

THE A-B-C PARADIGM

The A-B-C Paradigm is a cognitive technique that can be used to help individuals resolve problems.

I teach my clients that thought or cognition and emotion or feelings are closely interrelated. Therefore, as a consequence, how we feel and subsequently behave is basically determined by how we think — I use an A-B-C Paradigm to illustrate this process to clients of all ages. This approach is effective because most children and adults assume that behavior flows smoothly from A to B to C. For example:

A. Billy calls a client a name

B. The client becomes angry

C. The client hits Billy.

When I ask the child why did he hit Billy, he will almost always reply that he hit Billy because Billy called him a name that made him angry. I show the child that Billy's name calling did not make him mad; rather, what he told himself at point B (internalized self-verbalizations or thoughts) caused him to become angry, which then resulted in his hitting Billy. I ask the client, "If a much younger child called you the same name, would you become angry and hit him?" The client typically answers "no", because the younger child does not know what he is saying or doing. At this point I show the client that the same stimulus existed at A in his interaction with Billy and the younger child; in both cases he was called the same name. Thus, whether we become angry or not is determined by what we tell ourselves at B, which determines how we will behave at C. If we use rational thought processes at B (e.g., tell ourselves that an individual's statements regarding us at best represent this perceptions of us and not how we really are), the other person's behavior will have little effect on how we feel and behave. If the client does not make himself angry at B, by telling himself irrational things, he does not hit Billy and does not have to deal with the negative consequences (e.g., being disciplined by the school principal), which usually occurs when pupils fight in the school environment.

When adults seek therapy after they separate or divorce from their spouses, they are usually depressed. To assist them, I use the same example that I used with Billy, when asked, why they are depressed their answer is almost always, "because my wife or husband left me." I show them that the wife or husband leaving them is not why they are depressed, rather, it is what they are telling themselves at B (internalized self-verbalizations) that is making them depressed, because if he or she was in love with someone else, and wanted to live with that person. They would probably celebrate if their spouse left.

REFLECTIVE LISTENING

Reflective Listening is a cognitive technique in which a significant other communicates to a person that she recognizes the feelings that are associated with what he is saying. For example, your friend may say, "I hate my boss; he is unfair." To reflect your friend's feelings, you may say that it appears that you are angry and disappointed with how things are going at work. Reflective listening is an effective technique that can be used to assist a person in achieving problem resolution.

The three basic steps involved in effective problem resolution are:

1. First, reflect the person's feelings so that he or she feels understood.

2. Then help the person clarify the problem more precisely.

3. And third, help the person solve the problem he or she is confronted by:

   a. Exploring alternatives

   b. Assessing the consequences of alternatives; and

   c. Choosing modes of behavior that are self-enhancing rather than self-defeating.

Let us use the case of Johnny to illustrate how the three basic steps involved in the Reflective Listening process can be used to help others solve problems. Johnny, a 12-year-old, eighth grade student, very emotionally says to his mother, "I hate Mr. Brown! He's a mean teacher!"

STEP 1. REFLECTION: To reflect Johnny's feelings, his mother may say, "It appears that things are not going well in Mr. Brown's class."

For Teachers, Parents and Kids:

STEP 2. CLARIFICATION: Johnny may say, "Well, it's not really Mr. Brown who is the problem. It's Billy and Bobby who bug me in Mr. Brown's class."

STEP 3. RESOLUTION: Johnny's mother may say, "What do you think you can do to stop Billy and Bobby from bugging you in Mr. Brown's class?" Johnny can explore some alternatives.

For example: "I can skip Mr. Brown's class." or "I can ask Mr. Brown to assign me a desk that is not near Billy and Bobby." At that point, Johnny's mother may say, "What do you feel would happen if you skipped Mr. Brown's class?" By asking this she is assessing the consequences of alternatives. Johnny may say, "I would probably fail the course."

Going on, Johnny's mother may say. "What do you think would happen if you asked Mr. Brown to move your desk?"

Johnny may say, "He would probably move it. Then Billy and Bobby would not be able to bug me."

To help Johnny choose modes of behavior that are self-enhancing rather than self-defeating. Johnny's mother might then say, "What do you feel is best? What choice will work best for you?" Johnny would probably say, "To ask Mr. Brown to assign me a desk that is not near Billy and Bobby."

THE JIGSAW-PUZZLE TECHNIQUE

The Jigsaw-Puzzle Technique can be used by teachers to promote cooperation and enhance the self-esteem and achievement of their students. When using the Jigsaw-Puzzle Technique divide your class into small learning groups of five or six students each and set it up so that competitiveness would be incompatible with success. That is, create an environment in which students will have to cooperate with each other in order to succeed.

In this type of environment, the teacher is not the major source of knowledge; rather the assignments are structured in a fashion in which the students will have to treat each other as resources. To create this, provide each student with a piece of information which is vital to the completion of the assignment.

For example, if the assignment is to write an essay on the life of George Washington, the teacher may give one member of the group information regarding George Washington's life before he entered school; another member may be given information about him when he was in elementary school, whereas the third member of the group may receive information about his junior high years; the other members of the group may be given information about Washington's high school years, military years and political career. With this assignment, all members have to work together and rely on one another in order to complete the task successfully. With this strategy, the slowest member of the group is as essential as the brightest, because no one individual can experience success without the assistance of everyone in the group. This approach promotes cooperation and respect among group members.

To test the effectiveness of the Jigsaw-Puzzle Technique, Aronson and his colleagues in Austin, Texas studied elementary level students for six weeks and found that:

1. Children in the jigsaw groups liked their peers more at the end of the six weeks than did children in the traditional classrooms.

For Teachers, Parents and Kids:

2. Students in the jigsaw groups saw each other as learning resources: those in the traditional classroom did not.

3. Children in the jigsaw groups had stronger and more positive self-concepts at the end of the experiment; their self-esteem improved; and they felt increasingly more important in school, than did children in the traditional classrooms.

4. Children in the jigsaw groups not only felt better about themselves and liked their classmates better; they also generally appeared more accepting of themselves and others *(Aronson, 1979)*.

Teachers, parents and other care providers can also use the following strategies in their attempts to promote behavior self-control in the children and students in their care:

1. **POSITIVE REINFORCEMENT.** When teachers, parents and others provide a child positive reinforcement, they reward him or her (e.g., tokens that they can trade for treats; money; praise; opportunities to participate in self-selected activities) when they display appropriate behavior.

2. **PROMPTING.** When teachers, parents and others provide prompting they create an environment that increases the probability of the child displaying appropriate behavior (e.g., providing clear instructions; reminding the child to behave appropriately).

3. **TIME OUT.** When teachers, parents and others expose the child to time out, they isolate him or her from a classroom or home setting, that is reinforcing for him or her for displaying inappropriate behavior.

4. **RESPONSE COST.** When teachers, parents and others expose children to response cost, they remove rewards (e.g., 15 minutes from recess or gym) when they display inappropriate behavior.

SOURCE: Kazdin, 1980; Clarizio, 1980; Workman, 1982.

PARENTING POWER ORIENTED CHILDREN

When parenting children who display power and convey to you that you can't make them do anything they don't want to do, remember to:

1. Keep your cool

   use the

2. A-B-C Paradigm to control arousal;
   do not make yourself angry;

   When using the A-B-C Paradigm remember that:

What others say or do	A	Name calling
	⇩	
How you feel	B	Angry or Sad
	⇩	
What you say or do	C	Fight

3. Persevere ... Persevere ... Persevere
   - Don't give up; to assist your child you may have to persevere for weeks, months, years

   Also remember that

For Teachers, Parents and Kids:

4. When power is used effectively it can be beneficial to the child and can assist him/her in:

   a. maintaining personal autonomy and refusing to bow to peer pressure regarding:

- use of alcohol
- use of illegal drugs
- sexual behavior
- participating in violent acts against others
- association with individuals and groups who direct negative prejudice towards others.

DEALING WITH INAPPROPRIATE BEHAVIOR

The teacher in her attempts to extinguish inappropriate behavior can use:

1. **PLANNED IGNORING.** When using this technique, the teacher systematically ignores inappropriate behavior considered to be undesirable.

2. **SIGNAL INTERFACING.** This strategy employs non-verbal gestures such as eye contact and hand movements to communicate to the child that she is displeased with his or her behavior.

3. **SUPPORT THROUGH ROUTINE.** The teacher makes a concerted effort to provide consistency in interactions with the child in an attempt to encourage him to behave more appropriately.

ASSISTING BEHAVIORAL DISORDERED CHILDREN

Harve Rawson, Director of the Englishton Park Children's Centre has found the following strategies to be effective in assisting children who are experiencing Behavioral Problems:

1. **VERBAL PRAISE**
   - for example, immediately after a child emits a desirable behavior, tell him that you are pleased with his action. Verbal praise should be immediate and consistent.

2. **EXAGGERATED PHYSICAL GESTURES OF APPROVAL**
   - for example, when young children display desirable behavior, give them hugs; give junior high or high school students hi-5's, when they emit desirable behavior.

3. **RECOGNITION**
   - for example, provide children verbal and written recognition for their contributions.

4. **TOKEN ECONOMY SYSTEMS**
   - for example, provide tokens that children can "cash" in for "treats" or participation in self-selected activities for displaying desirable behavior.

5. **MODELING**
   - for example, the teacher, parent, therapist or other care providers models or displays desirable behavior. Modeling works because:
     - a) it shows the desirable, acceptable behavior visually.
     - b) it demonstrates that the desired act can be done.
     - c) it conveys the message that the act being modeled is not demeaning, degrading or embarrassing.

TEACHING BEHAVIORAL SELF-CONTROL: A PREVENTIVE MODEL

Prevention of conditions which impede development and the effective utilization of one's potential is an important goal for all caregivers who provide services for others. Some consequences of effective programs of prevention that promote self-esteem, academic achievement and behavioral self-control are:

- less crime
- lower rates of illegal and legal drug abuse
- lower incidences of teenage pregnancy
- fewer school dropouts or early leavers
- lower rates of violence
- fewer individuals requiring welfare benefits
- less expense
- more funds for human services
- more efficient use of human potential
- higher levels of mental health and well being
- empowerment, which increases participants' ability to emit behavior that is self-enhancing rather than self-defeating *(Battle, 1994)*

I recommend the following steps when teaching Behavior Self-Control:

STEP 1. Show the student how to use the A-B-C Paradigm to control arousal and emit behavior that is self-enhancing. When teaching A-B-C Paradigm use the following:

What others say or do	A	Name calling
	⇩	
How you feel	B	Angry
	⇩	
What you say or do	C	Fight

Show the student that the name calling at A cannot make him angry; rather what he tells himself at point B (internalized self-verbalizations or thoughts) about the name calling can make him angry and result in him fighting at C. *(see pp. 104-105).*

STEP II. Show the student how to use the technique of Reflective Listening to achieve problem resolution. The recommended sequence for teaching reflective listening is:

1. First, clarify the problem more precisely

  Then

2. Resolve the problem by:

  a. Exploring alternatives

  b. Assessing the consequences of alternatives

  And

  c. Choosing modes of behavior that are self-enhancing *(see pp.106-107).*

STEP III. Show the student how to use the ten questions procedure to assist him or her in emitting behavior that is enhancing: Encourage your student to ask him or her self the following questions when experiencing difficulties making decisions:

1. What is the worst thing that can happen if?

2. What is the best thing that can happen if?

3. How does this form of behavior help me?

4. How does this form of behavior hurt me?

5. What is the worst thing that can happen to me if others disapprove of my behavior?

6. What is the worst thing that can happen if others think bad things about me?

7. What alternatives or options do I have?

8. What are the probable consequences of the alternatives or options available to me?

9. What is the best thing for me to do?

10. What is the worst thing for me to do?

STEP IV. If the student emits behavior that is self-defeating and results in negative consequences, have him:

1. Determine what he did that resulted in him emitting behavior that is self-defeating.

2. Determine what he could have done to avoid emitting the behavior and having to deal with negative consequences.

3. Encourage the student to practice using:

- The A-B-C Paradigm
- Reflective Listening
- The Ten Questions Procedure
    To
- Assist him or her in controlling arousal and emitting behavior that is self-enhancing.

SUMMARY

1. Student and youth violence continues to escalate in schools and communities.

2. Self-esteem is probably the most important requirement for effective behavior control.

3. Attention-Deficit Hyperactive Disorder is a common behavioral problem of children and youth.

4. Many notable persons including Thomas Edison and Winston Churchill were considered to be hyperactive.

5. Conduct Disorders are commonly identified problems of children and youth.

6. Children experiencing behavioral problems should be provided clearly defined limits that are enforced consistently.

7. Teachers should set realistic, obtainable expectations for their students.

8. Teachers who set high expectations for their students obtain higher levels of academic performance than teachers who set low expectations.

9. Teachers' expectations can lead to a self-fulfilling prophecy.

10. Parents should provide their children structure and limits that are enforced consistently.

11. Teachers and Parents and other providers of care should promote the development of behavioral self-control in children and youth.

12. With appropriate behavioral self-control children can deliberately alter or change their behavior to achieve desired goals.

13. Self-assessment can be used to promote behavioral self-control.

14. Self-monitoring can be used to promote behavioral self-control.

15. Self-reinforcement can be used to promote behavioral self-control.

16. Problem resolution strategies can be used to promote self-esteem and behavioral self-control.

17. The A-B-C Paradigm is a cognitive technique that can be used to help kids and other individuals solve problems.

18. Reflective Listening is a cognitive technique that can be used to help kids and other individuals solve problems.

19. The Jigsaw-Puzzle Technique can be used to promote cooperation and enhance the self-esteem and achievement of students.

20. Strategies are available that can be used to assist in parenting power oriented children.

21. Preventive models can be used to teach behavioral self-control.

PART III

Recommended Reading
& Self-Esteem
Resource Materials

Recommended Reading

BOOKS AND PAPERS

ANDERSON, K. 1979. *The effects of the Magic Circle Program on the Self-Concepts of Children in Grades Four and Five.* Master's thesis. Edmonton, AB: University of Alberta.

> In this study, conducted as part of a master's thesis, the author investigates the effects that the Magic Circle Program has on the self-conceptions of participating students.

BATTLE, J. 1972. *The Effects of A Tutoring Program on the Self-Esteem and Academic Achievement of Elementary Students.* Doctoral dissertation. Edmonton, AB: University of Alberta.

> The author reports that fifth and sixth grade students who functioned as tutors of younger children experienced significant gains in spelling achievement.

BATTLE, J. 1990. *Enhancing Self-Esteem and Achievement.* Edmonton, AB: James Battle and Associates Ltd.

> The text provides a comprehensive overview of the phenomena that constitute self-esteem. How self-esteem and achievement interactions supplement each other is clearly delineated, and the author provides empirically tested strategies and techniques that enhance self-esteem and achievement. Twenty-six inventories that assess perception of self-worth are described.

BATTLE, J. 1990. *9 to 19: Crucial Years for Self-Esteem in Children and Youth*. Edmonton, AB: James Battle and Associates Ltd.

> In *9 to 19*, Dr. Battle identifies characteristics of positive and negative self-esteem, and traces the development of both dispositions. The important role that self-esteem plays in contemporary problems such as learning disabilities, conduct problems, anxiety disorders, depression and suicide is described. In *9 to 19*, Dr. Battle offers 110 strategies for remediating these and other problems. The effectiveness of these strategies are documented and actual case reports are provided to illustrate how positive shifts in self-esteem can be induced in students and clients. In the book, Dr. Battle offers concrete ways of identifying problems and acting to correct them, both in the classroom and in the home.

BATTLE, J. 1990. *Self-Esteem: the New Revolution*. Edmonton, AB: James Battle and Associates Ltd.

> In *Self-Esteem: The New Revolution*, Dr. Battle provides a comprehensive text that addresses the important issue of self-esteem. In the book the author offers 300 strategies that can be used to enhance the self-esteem of individuals at all developmental levels. Empirical data are provided to document the effectiveness of these strategies and actual case reports are presented to illustrate how positive shifts in self-esteem can be induced in individuals of all ages.

BATTLE, J. 1991. *Manual for Enhancing Self-Esteem: A Comprehensive Program of Strategies*. Edmonton, AB: James Battle and Associates Ltd.

For Teachers, Parents and Kids:

In this manual, Dr. Battle describes a program that has proven to be effective for enhancing the self-esteem of students and clients. The manual shows teacher show to use the video as an instructional aid. A list of examination questions and the key is also provided.

BATTLE, J. 1991. *Self-Esteem Research: A Summary of Relevant Findings.* Edmonton, AB: James Battle and Associates Ltd.

> *In Self-Esteem Research: A Summary of Relevant Findings,* Dr. Battle, documents research in the field of self-esteem and provides concise summaries of findings of research studies that addressed the construct.

BATTLE, J. 1992. *Explanations for Response Choice: A Guide for the Culture-Free Self-Esteem Inventories.* Edmonton, AB: James Battle and Associates Ltd.

> In this guide, Dr. Battle offers practical explanations for examinees response choices to each item of *The Culture-Free Self-Esteem Inventories for Children and Adults, Forms A, B and AD.*

BATTLE, J. 1992. *Self-esteem, Personality and Adjustment.* Edmonton, AB: James Battle and Associates Ltd.

> In this comprehensive text, Dr. Battle traces the origins of self-theory and self-esteem, personality and human adjustment. He documents how self-esteem and personality develops, and shows how both influence adjustment. Common adjustment failures are described and methodologies for alleviating these and other problems are delineated.

BATTLE, J. 1992. *Instructor's Manual for Self-Esteem, Personality and Adjustment*. Edmonton, AB: James Battle and Associates, Ltd.

This manual provides multiple choice, true and false and essay questions with keys for each.

BATTLE, J. 1993. *Misconceptions Regarding Self-Esteem*. Edmonton, AB: James Battle and Associates, Ltd.

Dr. Battle addresses a comprehensive number of misconceptions associated with the construct of self-esteem and offers factual information associated with each misconception. In addition, the author delineates specific strategies derived from empirical findings that practitioners can apply in real life settings to enhance self-esteem achievement and well-being.

BATTLE, J. 1994. *Promoting Self-Esteem, Achievement and Well Being: An Effective Instructional Curriculum for All Levels*. Edmonton, AB: James Battle and Associates Ltd.

In this practical book, Dr. Battle describes an instructional curriculum which incorporates more than 500 time-tested strategies that instructors can use to promote self-esteem, achievement and well being of students at all developmental levels.

BATTLE, J. 1994. *Strategies That You Can Use to Enhance Your Own Self-Esteem and Well Being*. Edmonton, AB: James Battle and Associates Ltd.

In this concise book, Dr. Battle describes strategies that individuals at all stages of development can use to enhance their own self-esteem, achievement and well-being.

BRANDEN, N. 1969. *The Psychology of Self-Esteem.* Los Angeles: Nash Publishing.
> The author presents the point of view which holds that self-esteem is a fundamental human need, and that various levels of self-esteem are consequences of our use of the freedom to think or not to think.

BRANDEN, N. 1980. *Breaking Free.* Los Angeles: Tharcher.
> The author offers 22 case reports that deal with the childhood origins of negative perceptions of self-worth.

BRANDEN, N. 1980. *The Disowned Self.* Los Angeles: Tharcher.
> Provides an overview of the problem of self-alienation.

BRIGGS, D.C. 1970. *Your Child's Self-Esteem.* Garden City, NY: Doubleday.
> This book gives an overview of self-esteem and offers suggestions for parents to promote self-esteem.

BROOKOVER, W.B., and THOMAS, S. 1964. *A Sociology of Education. 2nd ed.* New York: American Book Company.
> The authors provide data indicating a significant relationship between self-concept and achievement.

BURNS, R.B. 1979. *The Self-Concept in Theory, Measurement, Development, and Behavior.* London: Longman.
> The author proposes that the self-concept is the composite image of what we think we are, what we think we can achieve, what we think others think of us, and what we would like to do.

COOPERSMITH, S. 1967. *Antecedents of Self-Esteem.* San Francisco: W. H. Freeman.
> The author examines antecedents that contribute to the development of high self-esteem.

CUMMINGS, R.N. 1971. *A Study of the Relationship Between Self-Concepts and Reading Achievement at the Third Grade Level.* Doctoral dissertation. University of Alabama. Microfilm. Ann Arbor, MI: University Microfilms.

> Findings of the study indicate that self-concept is significantly related to reading achievement.

DINKMEYER, D., and DREIKURS, R. 1963. *Encouraging Children to Learn: The Encouragement Process.* Englewood Cliffs, New Jersey: Prentice-Hall.

> Solutions to problem-solving in this text, emphasize encouragement in the learning process and de-emphasize conflict and confrontation.

HAMACHEK, D.E. 1971. *Encounters with Self.* New York: Holt, Rinehart and Winston.

> Here, awareness of self begins at birth; self-perception is determined, in part, by how we perceive ourselves as really being, how we ideally perceive ourselves, and how we feel others perceive us.

HAMACHEK, D.E. 1978. *Encounters with Self.* New York: Holt, Rinehart, and Winston.

> The author discusses various components of the self and describes how a healthy self-concept develops.

JERSILD, A.T. 1952. *In Search of Self.* New York: Teachers College Press.

> According to the author, schools should take an active role in promoting self understanding.

LABENNE, W.D., and GREEN, B.I. 1969. *Educational Implications of Self-Concept Theory.* Pacific Palisades, CA: Goodyear Publishing.

> Gives an overview of self-concept theory and offers views regarding how information derived from self-concept theory can promote educational advances.

MURPHY, G. 1975. *Outgrowing Self-Deception.* New York: Basic Books.

    The author examines the human need to perceive the self as worthy, and how people may strive to protect themselves from negative self-feeling through self-deception.

PATERSON, K.M. 1980. *An Investigation of Self-Esteem and Related Variables of Educationally Mentally Handicapped Students.* Master's thesis. Edmonton, AB: University of Alberta.

    The study reports findings which indicate that the self-esteem of mentally retarded students is significantly related to teachers' ratings of their behavior.

PURKEY, W.W. 1970. *Self-Concept and School Achievement.* Englewood Cliffs, NJ: PrenticeHall.

    The book gives an historical review of the various theories that deal with the self, and lists characteristics of the self.

RAIMY, V. 1975. *Misunderstandings of The Self.* San Francisco: Jossey-Bass.

    The author offers a "misconception" hypothesis, in which he indicates that people can resolve emotional problems by eliminating faulty ideas and beliefs.

ROSENBERG, M. 1979. *Conceiving The Self.* New York: Basic Books.

    The author describes an individual's frame of reference, or the foundation on which actions are predicated, and proposes that self-esteem and self-consistency are distinct motives which guide human behaviour.

SAMUELS, S.C. 1977. *Enhancing Self-Concept in Early Childhood: Theory and Practice.* New York: Human Sciences.

This book proposes that early childhood is the most critical period for the development of self-concept, and that a key goal of parents and teachers of children under the age of six should be to enhance their perceptions of self worth.

SIMON, N. 1976. *Why Am I Different?* New York: A. Whitman.

Realistic self-image is essential for positive psychological growth.

SNYGG. D., and COMBS, A.W. 1959. *Individual Behaviour.* New York: Harper and Row.

The fundamental thesis of this book is that the perceptual field of each human being determines his or her behaviour in every instance.

THOMAS, J.B. 1973. *Self-Concept in Psychology and Education: A Review of Research.* New York: Humanities Press.

The book presents the position that the self is a learned structure that is more influenced by interactions with parents and other family members than it is by social class.

WYLIE, R. 1961. *The Self-Concept: A Critical Survey of Pertinent Research Literature.* Lincoln, NE: University of Nebraska Press.

The book reviews research regarding the self-concept which was conducted prior to 1961.

YANIW, L. 1983. *The Relationship Between Three Affective Variables and Student Achievement.* Master's thesis. Edmonton, AB: University of Alberta.

The study reports findings which confirm that achievement is related to self-esteem, and that this relationship appears to be fairly independent of measured intelligence.

For Teachers, Parents and Kids:

ARTICLES, PRESENTATIONS, AND REPORTS

BATTLE, J. 1978. *Relationship Between Self-Esteem and Depression.* PSYCHOLOGICAL REPORTS 42:745-746.
> Findings confirm the relationship between self-esteem and depression in adults is significant: as depression intensifies, self-esteem diminishes.

BATTLE, J. 1980. *Relationship Between Self-Esteem and Depression Among High School Students.* PERCEPTUAL AND MOTOR SKILLS 51:157-158.
> Findings confirm the relationship between self-esteem and depression in adolescents is significant.

BATTLE, J. 1981. *Enhancing Self-Esteem: A New Challenge to Teachers.* ACADEMIC THERAPY (May) 16:5, pp. 541-550.
> The article delineates the important role that self-esteem plays in the educative process, and encourages teachers to accept the challenge of addressing both cognitive and affective needs of pupils.

BATTLE, J. 1983. *The Teacher's Role in the Enhancement of Self-Esteem and Achievement.* PRIME AREAS (Winter) 25:2.
> Teachers can exert a strong effect on their students' self-esteem: the author encourages teachers to interact positively with students.

BATTLE, J. 1984. *Relationship Between Self-Esteem and Depression Among Children.* Edmonton, AB: Edmonton Public Schools.
> The data reported indicate that the relationship between self-esteem and depression in children is similar to that of adolescents and adults.

BATTLE, J. 1991. *No Strings Attached.* ALBERTA PARENTS MAGAZINE. March/April.

> Common goals of children's misbehaviour are identified and parents are shown how to interact with their children and assist them in developing their potential more fully.

BATTLE, J. 1993. *Kids and Self-Esteem: A Role for Teachers.* WELL SPRING MAGAZINE. February.

> The article states that enhancing student self-esteem is an important challenge for teachers and describes strategies that teachers can use to promote the self-esteem, achievement and well being of their pupils.

BATTLE, J. 1993. *Ex-Football Star Preaches Self-Esteem.*

> The article states that most problems students have in school are associated with low self-esteem and dispels common misconceptions such as low self-esteem is a problem basically of economically disadvantaged individuals and groups.

BATTLE, J. and BLOWERS, T.G. 1982. *A Longitudinal Comparative Study of the Self-Esteem of Students in Regular and Special Classes.* JOURNAL OF LEARNING DISABILITIES (February) 15:2.

> Self-esteem of learning-disabled and regular students is compared; effects that special class placement have on learning-disabled students over a three-year period are described.

BATTLE, J., JARRETT, L., SINHA, S., and PRECHT, D. 1988. *Relations Among Self-Esteem, Depression and Anxiety of Children.* PSYCHOLOGICAL REPORTS 62: 999-1005.

> Findings confirm the relationship between self-esteem, depression and anxiety in children.

For Teachers, Parents and Kids:

BATTLE, J. and YANISH, D.L., 1985. *Relationship Between Self-Esteem, Depression and Alcohol Consumption Among Adolescents.* PSYCHOLOGICAL REPORTS 57: 331-334.

> Findings cited here confirm previous observations that indicate that self-esteem and depression are significantly related; alcohol consumption is associated with the various facets of self-esteem as measured by *the Culture-Free Self-Esteem Inventory for Children.*

BEANE, J. 1973. *Self-Concept and Self-Esteem as Curriculum Issues.* TODAY'S EDUCATION (NEA JOURNAL).

> The author proposes that one's concept of ability influences achievement; achievement, in turn, influences one's concept of ability.

CAMPBELL, L. 1981. *Improving Self-Image.* North Texas State University NASSD BULLETIN (Denton).

> The author argues that negative self-concept is the most crucial variable impeding academic achievement in students, preventing them from developing their full potential.

CHARALAMPOUS, K.D., FORD, K.F., and SKINNER, T.J. 1976. *Self-Esteem in Alcoholics and Non-Alcoholics.* JOURNAL OF STUDIES ON ALCOHOL 37:990-994.

> Findings indicate that alcoholism is associated with low levels of self-esteem.

FAHEY, M., and PHILLIPS, S. 1981. *The Self-Concept in Middle Childhood: Some Baseline Data.* CHILD STUDY JOURNAL 11:3, pp. 155-165.

> The thesis holds that self-concept grows or develops during middle childhood.

KIDWELL, J. 1982. *The Neglected Birth Order: Middleborns.* JOURNAL OF MARRIAGE AND THE FAMILY pp. 225-235.

Reported findings indicate that middleborn children possess lower levels of self-esteem than first or last-born children.

MITIC, W.R. 1980. *Alcohol Use and Self-Esteem of Adolescents.* JOURNAL OF DRUG EDUCATION 10: 197-208.

Data reported indicate that individuals who drink alcohol on a regular basis possess significantly lower levels of self-esteem than those who do not drink.

RAWSON, H.E. 1992. *The Interrelationship of Measures of Manifest Anxiety, Self-Esteem, Locus of Control and Depression in Children with Behaviour Problems.* JOURNAL OF PSYCHOEDUCATIONAL ASSESSMENT. 10, 319-329.

Findings of the study indicate that self-esteem correlated significantly and negatively with depression and anxiety, but had little correlation with external locus of control.

STAINES, J.W. 1958. *The Development of Children's Values: The Self-Picture as A Factor in the Classroom.* BRITISH JOURNAL OF EDUCATIONAL PSYCHOLOGY 18:97-111.

The article delineates the important effects that self-esteem has in behaviour and achievement. The author says that the self is the major component of the personality, and encourages teachers to make concerted efforts to improve the self-perceptions of their pupils.

STEVENSON, D.T., and Romney, D.M. 1984. *Depression in Learning-Disabled Children.* JOURNAL OF LEARNING DISABILITIES 10:579-582.

The article gives data supporting the position that self-esteem is significantly associated with depression in children.

WATSON, J. 1973. *How to Change Negative Self-Concepts in Low-Ability Children*. TODAY'S EDUCATION (NEA JOURNAL) pp. 26-27.

Strategies are offered for teachers to use in improving the self-concepts of children with low ability.

WATTENBURG, M.W. and CLIFFORD, C. 1964. *Relationship of Self-Concepts to Beginning Achievement in Reading*. CHILD DEVELOPMENT 35:461-467.

The study indicates that positive self-concept is an antecedent of reading and that self-concept scores can be used to predict subsequent reading achievement.

Self-Esteem
Resource Materials

BOOKS

AMINAH, C., HARRIS, C., and REYNOLDS, B. 1987. *How to Raise Teenagers' Self-Esteem*. Los Angeles: Enrich.

BARKSDALE, L.S. 1977. *Essays on Self-Esteem*. Idyllwilde, CA.: The Barksdale Foundation.

BATTLE, J. 1990. *Enhancing Self-Esteem and Achievement*. Edmonton: James Battle and Associates Ltd.

BATTLE, J. 1990. *Self-Esteem: The New Revolution*. Edmonton: James Battle and Associates Ltd.

BATTLE, J. 1992. *Self-Esteem, Personality and Adjustment*. Edmonton: James Battle and Associates Ltd.

BATTLE, J. 1991. *Self-Esteem Research: A Summary of Relevant Findings*. Edmonton: James Battle and Associates Ltd.

BATTLE, J. 1992. *Explanations for Response Choice: A Guide for The Culture-Free Self-Esteem Inventories*. Edmonton: James Battle and Associates Ltd.

BATTLE, J. 1990. *9 To 19: Crucial Years for Self-Esteem in Children and Youth*. Edmonton: James Battle and Associates Ltd.

BATTLE, J. 1992. *Manual for Enhancing Self-Esteem: A Comprehensive Program of Strategies*. Edmonton: James Battle and Associates Ltd.

BATTLE, J. 1993. *Misconceptions Regarding Self-Esteem.* Edmonton: James Battle and Associates, Ltd.

BORBA, M., and BORBA, C. 1982. *Self-Esteem: The Classroom Affair* (Vol.2). San Francisco: Harper & Row.

BORBA, M. 1989. *Esteem Builders.* Rolling Hills Estates, Winch and Associates: Jalmar Press.

BRIGGS, D.C. 1970. *Your Child's Self-Esteem.* Garden City, NY: Doubleday.

BRIGGS, D.C. 1977. *Celebrate Yourself.* Garden City, NY: Doubleday.

CLEMES, H., and BEAN, R. 1981. *Self-Esteem: The Key to Your Child's Well-Being.* New York: Putman.

COOPERSMITH, S.R. 1967. *The Antecedents of Self-Esteem.* San Francisco: W.H. Freeman:

COOPERSMITH, S.R., and SILVERMAN, J. 1969. *How to Enhance Pupil Self-Esteem.* Today's Education.

COVINGTON, M., and Beery, R. 1976. *Self-Worth and School Learning.* New York: Holt, Rinehart and Winston.

DINKMEYER, D. 1970. *Developing an Understanding of Self and Others* (DUSO). Circle Pines, MN: American Guidance Service.

FORTE, L. 1978. *Self-Esteem: A Classroom Affair: 101 Ways to Help Children like Themselves.* Minneapolis: Winston.

HARRIS, C., and REYNOLD, B. 1987. *How to Raise Children's Self-Esteem.* Los Angeles: Enrich.

PINKEY, W.W. 1970. *Self-Concept and School Achievement.* Englewood Cliffs, NJ: Prentice Hall.

RANDOLPH, N., and HOWE, W. 1966. *Self-Enhancing Education.* Palo Alto, CA: Stanford University Press.

ROSENTHAL, R., and JACOBSON, L. 1968. *Pygmalion in the Classroom: Teacher Expectation and Pupils' Intellectual Development.* New York: Holt, Rinehart and Winston.

SCHULLER, R.C. 1982. *Self-esteem: The New Reformation.* Waco, TX: Word Books Inc.

SEARS, P. 1964. *In Pursuit of Self-Esteem.* Belmont, CA.: Wadsworth.

WELLS, H.C., and CANFIELD, J. 1976. *One Hundred Ways to Enhance Self-Concept in the Classroom.* Englewood Cliffs, NJ: Prentice Hall.

WHITE, E. 1980. *Nourishing the Seeds of Self-Esteem.* Capitola, CA: Whitenwife Publications.

TAPES

BATTLE, J. *Effective Parenting Tips that Build Self-Esteem, Revised.* James Battle and Associates Ltd., #406, Edwards Building, 10053 111 Street, Edmonton, AB T5K 2H8.

BATTLE, J. *Strategies You Can Use to Enhance Your Own Self-Esteem.* James Battle and Associates, #406, Edwards Building, 10053 -111 Street, Edmonton, AB T5K 2H8.

CANFIELD, J. *Self-esteem in the Classroom.* Self-Esteem Seminars. Pacific Palisades, CA.

MALONEY, M.A. and STEELE, B. *The Self-Esteem Connection.* Published by Ann Arbor Publishers, P.O. Box 7249, Naples, FL. 33491.

VIDEO

BATTLE, J. 1992. *Enhancing Self-Esteem: A Comprehensive Program of Strategies.*

James Battle and Associates Ltd.
#406, Edwards Building,
10053 111 Street,
Edmonton, AB Canada T5K 2H8

POEMS

BATTLE, J. 1992. *Self-Esteem Poems.*
James Battle and Associates Ltd., #406, Edwards Building, 10053 111 Street, Edmonton, AB T5K 2H8.
The complete set of poems include:
1. The Self-Esteem Poem, 2. Children: Important Resources, 3. Children: You and Me, 4. My Mom and Dad, 5. Then I Reflected and Thanked My God.

PROGRAMS

PROJECT SELF-ESTEEM - SANDY MCDANIEL, PEGGY BIELEN
A parent involvement program for elementary-age children.
Published by: B.L. Winch & Associates
45 Hitching Post Drive, Building 2
Rolling Hills Estates, CA 90274

SELF-ESTEEM IN THE CLASSROOM - JACK CANFIELD
Compiled by: Self-Esteem Seminars
17156 Palisades Circle
Pacific Palisades, CA 90272

BUILDING SELF-ESTEEM - *Teacher's Guide and Classroom Materials* - ROBERT W. REASONER
Published by: Consulting Psychologists Press, Inc.
577 College Avenue
Palo Alto, CA 94306

HOW TO RAISE CHILDREN'S SELF-ESTEEM - CLARK, A., HARRIS, M.A., CLEMES, H., AND BEAN, R.
Published by: Price/Stern/Sloan Publishers, Inc.
410 North La Cienega Boulevard
Los Angeles, CA 90048

BUILDING SELF-ESTEEM - *Administrator's Guide, Second Edition* - ROBERT W. REASONER
> Published by: Consulting Psychologists Press, Inc.
> 577 College Avenue
> Palo Alto, CA 94306

BUILDING SELF-ESTEEM - *Parent's Guide* - ROBERT W. REASONER
> Published by: Consulting Psychologists Press, Inc.
> 577 College Avenue
> Palo Alto, CA 4306

ESTEEM BUILDERS: *A K-8 Self-Esteem Curriculum for Improving Student Achievement, Behavior and Climate* - MICHELE BORBA
> Published by: B.L. Winch and
>   Associates/Jalmar Press
> 45 Hitchings Post Drive, Building 2
> Rolling Hills Estates, CA 90274

ENHANCING SELF-ESTEEM: *A Comprehensive Program of Strategies* - JAMES BATTLE.
> Published by: James Battle and Associates Ltd.
> #406, Edwards Building
> 10053 111 Street
> Edmonton, AB T5K 2H8

ENGLISHTON PARK ACADEMIC REMEDIATION AND TRAINING PROGRAM
A summer camp program for children aged 8 to 12 years.
> Sponsored by: The United Presbyterian Ministries
> Director: Harve Rawson, Ph.D.
> Hanover College, Hanover, IN 47243

SELF-ESTEEM INSTITUTE OF CANADA
>President: James Battle, Ph.D.
>#406 Edwards Building
>10053 - 111 Street
>Edmonton, Alberta, Canada
>T5K 2H8

A COMPREHENSIVE PROGRAM OF INSTRUCTION FOR DISABLED READERS
>Developed by: STEVEN TRUCH, PH.D.
>The Reading Foundation
>#250, 200 Rivercrest Drive, S.E.
>Calgary, AB T2C 2X5

WHAM: WHAT ABOUT ME -PATRICK TRUSIO
>Published by: Patrick Trusio, Inc.
>#1073, 8011 North 7th Street
>Phoenix, AR 85020

Self-Esteem Institute of Canada

The Self-Esteem Institute of Canada is an organization comprised of individuals who are dedicated to promoting the self-esteem and well being of all persons:

Our
Philosophy:

The Self-Esteem Institute of Canada recognizes and appreciates the inherent worth of all persons; and, recognizes the important role that self-esteem plays in the lives of individuals at all stages of their development and, is dedicated to promoting the self-esteem and well being of all persons.

Vision:

Our Vision is that every person have the opportunity to establish and maintain a sense of personal worth and self-esteem throughout their entire life.

Mission:

Our Mission is to promote the self-esteem and well being of all individuals through accessible programs and services.

James Battle, Ph.D. - *President*

Frank Saulnier - *Chairman of the Advisory Board*

ADDRESS ALL CORRESPONDENCE TO:

Self-Esteem Institute of Canada

#406 Edwards Building, 10053 - 111 Street
Edmonton, Alberta, Canada   T5K 2H8
Ph. (403) 488-1362   •   Fax (403) 482-3332   •   1-800-463-9144

PART IV

Glossary of Terms
References & Indexes

Glossary of Terms

A

ACADEMIC SELF-ESTEEM: An individual's perception of his or her ability to succeed academically

ACHIEVEMENT: Level of information acquired in a given area of knowledge

ACHIEVEMENT TEST: A measure of what has been acquired in a given area of knowledge

ADJUSTMENT: A satisfactory state of functioning

ANXIETY DISORDER: A condition characterized by irrational apprehension

APTITUDE: Ability or capacity to learn certain tasks

ATTENTION-DEFICIT HYPERACTIVITY DISORDER: A condition characterized by an inability to sustain attention appropriately

AUTHENTIC: Real, genuine

AVERAGE: Measure of central tendency

B

BEHAVIOR MAINTENANCE: Maintaining desireable behavior

BIOGENIC: Due to biological factors

C

CHRONOLOGICAL AGE: Actual age

CORRELATION: The tendency of certain arrays of frequency distributions to be positively, negatively, or not at all associated

Cognitive: The mental process or faculty of knowing

D

DEPRESSION: An emotional disorder characterized by difficulties concentrating or a despondent mood

DEVIATION: The amount by which a score deviates from the measure of central tendency

DIGIT SPAN: The number of correlated digits correctly reproduced after a single presentation

E

ENCOURAGEMENT: To inspire, spur and support another

EXPERIMENT: A controlled application of the empirical method of inquiry in which the investigator varies one factor at a time for the purposes of testing an hypothesis

F

FACTOR ANALYSIS: A procedure for analyzing the inter-correlations among arrays of scores in order to determine those factors involved

FANTASY: DAY DREAMING: the individual creates an imaginary world in order to gratify his needs

FEEDBACK: A procedure which provides an individual insights regarding his behavior

FREQUENCY SELF-MONITORING: A procedure in which an individual records the number of times she engages in a given form of behavior.

G

GENERAL SELF-ESTEEM: An individual's general perception of his or her worth

H

HYPOTHESIS: A proposition which is empirically tested to determine whether or not it is valid

For Teachers, Parents and Kids:

I

INTELLIGENCE QUOTIENT: A score derived from performance on standardized tests of intelligence - commonly referred to as IQ

INTERNAL SELF-MONITORING: A procedure in which an individual records the number of time intervals he engages in a certain form of behavior

INTROJECTION: Taking on someone's personality dispositions

J

JUNIOR HIGH STRATEGIES: Strategies for students in junior high or middle school

M

MEAN: The arithmetical average; $m = \dfrac{(x)}{n}$

MUTUAL RESPECT: Mutuality and respect for others

N

NORMAL: The value representing an average

O

OBTAINED SCORE: The value before statistical treatment is given

P

PARENT SELF-ESTEEM: An individual's perception of his status at home with his parents

PERCENTILE RANK: The relative position of each score in the distribution as arranged on a scale of one hundred

PERSONALITY: Characteristics that distinguish one individual from others

PERSONAL SELF-ESTEEM: An individual's most intimate perception of self-worth

PROFILE: A graphic representation of an individual's test scores

PSYCHOGENIC: Traceable to psychological or environmental experiences

PSYCHOTHERAPY: A general term for psychological treatment procedures

PSEUDO: Not real, non genuine

Q

QUOTIENT: The number obtained by dividing one number by another number

R

RANDOM SAMPLE: A number of persons or objects drawn by chance from a larger population, generally on the assumption they will represent the larger group

RANGE: Difference between the largest and smallest value in a distribution

RATING: Estimating on some systematic basis, the presence or absence or the magnitude of some trait, characteristic or quality of person, thing or process

REFLECTION: A therapeutic technique in which the therapist clarifies the patient's feelings by interpreting the emotional tone of his remarks

RELIABILITY: The extent to which a measurement device measures whatever it purports to measure

RESULTS: The outcome of an empirical investigation upon which the conclusions are based

S

SAMPLE: A group of subjects participating in a research study

SELF-ACTUALIZATION: The realization of one's inherent potentials

For Teachers, Parents and Kids:

SELF-CONCEPT: The totality of perceptions an individual has and customarily maintains regarding himself or herself

SELF-CONTROL: A process in which an individual deliberately alters her behavior

SELF-DISCLOSURE: The act of opening up; making oneself transparent to others

SELF-ESTEEM: An individual's perception of his or her own worth

SELF-IMAGE: An individual's perception of his or her own traits

SELF-INSTRUCTION: Using verbalizations to instruct oneself

SELF-MONITORING: A procedure in which an individual monitors his own behavior

SELF-PERPETUATION: Pertaining to the disposition to accentuate and intensify traits that are already present in oneself

SELF-RATING: Rating one's own behavior

SELF-REPORT INVENTORY: An objective check list or inventory

SOCIAL SELF-ESTEEM: An individual's perception of interpersonal interactions

STANDARD DEVIATION: The square root of the deviations squared from the mean distribution (in a normal frequency distribution, the middle 68.34 percent of the scores)

STANDARDIZATION: The creation of uniform conditions

STANINES: Units dividing the population into nine groups ranging from 1 to 9 with a mean of 5

STATISTICS: The application of techniques of mathematics to the treatment of data

SUBJECTIVE: Not directly observable by another person but accessible through the individual's own verbal report or introspection

SUB-TEST: A logical division of a test

SURROGATE PARENT: Substitute parent

T

T-SCORE: A score on a 100-unit scale with a mean of 50 and a standard deviation of 10

TEST: Any technique for validating or invalidating any hypothesis

TEST BATTERY: A group of tests

TESTEE: Examinee or person being tested

TEST ITEMS: Items that comprise a test

TEST PROFILE: A graphic display of test findings

THERAPY: Generic term that refers to treatment of disorders

TOTAL SELF-ESTEEM: A composite score; for children, derived from general, social academic and parent facets; for adults, derived from general, social and personal facets

U

UNCONDITIONED POSITIVE REGARD: Caring that is not contingent on behaviour

V

VALIDITY: The extent to which an instrument measures what it purports to measure

VARIABLE: A trait on which events or people differ

W

WECHSLER ADULT INTELLIGENCE SCALE (WAIS-Revised): Comprehensive test of intelligence for males and females 16 years and older

WECHSLER INTELLIGENCE SCALE FOR CHILDREN: Revised
(WISC-R): Comprehensive test of intelligence for boys
and girls aged 6 through 16

Z

ZERO CORRELATION: A lack of any association between two
distributions of scores

References

ADLER, A. *The Practice and Therapy of Individual Psychology.* New York: Harcourt. 1927.

ALLEN, U.L., AND FELDMAN, R.S. *Learning Through Tutoring: Low Achieving Children as Tutors.* TECHNICAL REPORT NO. 236. Madison, Wisconsin: University of Wisconsin. 1972.

ARONSON, E. *The Need For Achievement as Measured By Graphic Expression.* JOURNAL OF GENETIC PSYCHOLOGY. 4814 - 49, 1988.

ARONSON, E, BLANEY, N., SIKES, J., STEPHANS, C. AND SNAPP, M. *Busing and Racial Tension: The Jigsaw Route to Learning and Liking.* PSYCHOLOGY TODAY (February) pp. 43 - 50.

BATTLE, J. *The Relationship Between Intelligence and Self-Esteem.* Edmonton, Alberta: Edmonton Public Schools. 1972.

BATTLE, J. *Comparative Study of the Self-Esteem of Deviant and Non-Deviant Students.* Edmonton, Alberta: Edmonton Public Schools. 1975.

BATTLE, J. *Relationship Between Self-Esteem and Depression.* PSYCHOLOGICAL REPORTS, 42:745-746. 1978.

BATTLE, J. *Self-esteem of Students in Regular and Special Classes.* PSYCHOLOGICAL REPORTS, 42:212-214. 1979.

BATTLE, J. *Culture-free Self-Esteem Inventories for Children and Adults.* SEATTLE: SPECIAL CHILD PUBLICATIONS. 1981 a.

BATTLE, J. *Enhancing Self-Esteem: A New Challenge to* Teachers. Academic Therapy (May), 16:5, pp. 541-550. 1981.

BATTLE, J. *Misconceptions Regarding Self-Esteem.* Edmonton, Alberta: James Battle And Associates, Ltd. 1993.

BATTLE, J. *The Teacher's Role in the Enhancement of Self-Esteem and Achievement.* PRIME AREAS (Winter), 24:2. 1983.

BATTLE, J. *Relationship Between Self-Esteem and Depression Among Children.* Edmonton: Edmonton Public Schools. 1984.

BATTLE, J. *Effective Parenting Tips That Build Self-Esteem.* SEATTLE; SPECIAL CHILD PUBLICATIONS. 1985.

BATTLE, J. *The Effects That Systematic Intervention Have on the Self-Esteem of Little Sisters.* Paper prepared for the Big Sisters Society of Edmonton. Edmonton, Alberta, Canada. 1985.

BATTLE, J. *Enhancing the Self-Esteem of Students.* Presentation at the Fourth Annual Self-Esteem Conference of the Self-Esteem Institute. Santa Clara, CA. 1987.

BATTLE, J. *Test-Retest Reliability of Battle's Depression Inventory for Children.* PSYCHOLOGICAL REPORTS, 61:71-74. 1987.

BATTLE, J. *The Effects That Junior Leadership Programs Have on Self-Esteem, Depression and Behaviour of Adolescents.* Paper prepared for the Boys' and Girls' Clubs of Edmonton. Edmonton, Alberta, Canada. 1988.

BATTLE, J. *Test-Retest Reliability of Battle's Anxiety Scale for Children.* PSYCHOLOGICAL REPORTS, 63:127-130. 1988.

BATTLE, J. *Enhancing Self-Esteem and Achievement.* Edmonton, Alberta: James Battle and Associates Ltd. 1990.

BATTLE, J. *9 to 19: Crucial Years for Self-Esteem in Children and Youth.* Edmonton, Alberta: James Battle and Associates Ltd. 1990.

For Teachers, Parents and Kids:

BATTLE, J. *Self-Esteem: The New Revolution.* Edmonton, Alberta: James Battle and Associates, Ltd. 1990.

BATTLE, J. *Self-Esteem Personality and Adjustment.* Edmonton, Alberta: James Battle and Associates, Ltd. 1992.

BATTLE, J. *Self-Esteem Poems.* Edmonton, Alberta: James Battle and Associates, Ltd. 1992.

BATTLE, J. *Explanations for Response Choice: A Guide For the Culture-Free Self- Esteem Inventories.* Edmonton, Alberta: James Battle and Associates, Ltd. 1992.

BATTLE, J. *Enhancing Self-Esteem: A Comprehensive Program of Strategies.* Edmonton, Alberta: James Battle and Associates, Ltd. 1992.

Battle, J. *Manual for Enhancing Self-Esteem: A Comprehensive Program of Strategies.* Edmonton, Alberta: James Battle and Associates, Ltd. 1992.

BATTLE, J. *Instructor's Manual For Self-Esteem, Personality and Adjustment.* Edmonton, Alberta: James Battle and Associates, Ltd. 1992.

BATTLE, J. *Culture-Free Self-Esteem Inventories for Children and Adults.* Austin: Pro Ed. 1992.

BATTLE, J. *The North American Self-Esteem Inventories For Children and Adults.* Edmonton: James Battle and Associates, Ltd. 1992.

BATTLE, J. *The Anxiety Scales for Children and Adults.* Austin: Pro Ed. 1993.

BATTLE, J. *Promoting Self-Esteem, Achievement and Well Being: An Effective Instructional Curriculum for All Levels.* Edmonton, AB: James Battle and Associates, Ltd. 1994.

BATTLE, J. *Strategies That You Can Use to Enhance Your Own Self-Esteem and Well Being.* Edmonton, AB: James Battle and Associates, Ltd. 1994.

BATTLE, J., and LACEY, B.A. *Context for Hyperactivity in Children Over Five.* CHILD DEVELOPMENT. 43:757-773. 1972.

BATTLE, J., and MESTON, J. *A Longitudinal Comparative Study of the Self-Esteem of Students in Regular and Special Classes.* JOURNAL OF LEARNING DISABILITIES. Vol. 15, No. 2, February. 1976.

BATTLE, J., AND BLOWERS, T. *A Longitudinal Comparative Study of the Self-Esteem of Students in Regular and Special Classes.* JOURNAL OF LEARNING DISABILITIES. Vol. 15, No. 2, February. 1980.

BATTLE, J., AND ANDRIASHEK, S. *The Effects of Partial Mainstreaming on the Self-Esteem of Special Education Students.* Edmonton, Alberta: Edmonton Public Schools. 1980.

BATTLE, J., JARRATT, L., SINHA, S. AND PRECHT, D. *The Relations Among Self-Esteem, Depression and Anxiety of Children.* PSYCHOLOGICAL REPORTS. 62, 999-1005. 1988.

BATTLE, J. AND SHEA, R. *Relationship Between Attention Deficit Hyperactivity Disorder and Self-Esteem.* Edmonton, Alberta, Canada. 1989.

BORBA, M. *Esteem Builders.* Rolling Hills Estates, Winch and Associates/Jalmar Press. 1989.

BRANDEN, N. *The Psychology of Self-Esteem.* New York: Bantam Books. 1971.

BRANDEN, N. *If You Could Hear What I Can Not Say.* New York: Bantam Books. 1983.

BRANDEN, N. *Honoring the Self.* Bantam Books: New York. 1983.

BRIGGS, D.C. *Your Child's Self-Esteem.* Garden city, New York. Doubleday. 1970.

CANFIELD, J., and Wells, H.C. *One hundred Ways to Enhance Self-Concept in the Classroom: A Handbook for Teachers and Parents.* Englewood Cliffs, NJ: Prentice Hall. 1976.

COHEN, A.R. *Some Implications of Self-Esteem for Social Influence.* C.I. Howland and I.L. Janis (Eds.) PERSONALITY AND PERSUABILITY, (pp.102-120). New Haven: Yale University Press. 1957.

COMBS, A.W. AND SNYGG, D. *New Horizons in Field Research: The Self-Concept.* EDUCATIONAL LEADERSHIP, 15:313 - 319, 1958.

COOPERSMITH, S. *Antecedents of Self-Esteem.* San Francisco: W.H. Freeman, 1967.

CORBETT, C. *The Hidden Unemployable.* Winnipeg, Manitoba. 1985.

DEPAUW, J. *Keeping Children in School: Springfield's District Wide Prevention and Intervention Program for All At Risk Students.* Assoc. Bulletin, April. 1987.

DINKMEYER, D., AND DINKMEYER, D., Jr. DUSO: *Developing Understanding of Self and Others.* Circle Pines, Minnesota: American Guidance Service. 1982.

DINKMEYER, D., AND MCKAY, M. *Systematic Training for Effective Parenting: Parents' Handbook.* Circle Pines, Minnesota: American Guidance Service. 1976.

DREIKURS, R.; GRUNWALD, B.B.; AND PEPPER, F.C. *Maintaining Sanity in the Classroom.* New York: Harper. 1971.

GLAZER, S.M. AND SEARFOSS, L.W. *Reading Diagnosis and Instruction: A C-A-L-M Approach.* Englewood Cliffs, N.J. Prentice-Hall, 1988, p. 220.

FRAGER, A.J., AND STERN, C. *Learning by Teaching.* THE READING TEACHER 23:5, pp 403- 406. 1970.

JEVINE, R.F.J AND ZINGLE, H.W.S. *Striving For Health: Living With Broken Dreams.* Edmonton. The Alberta School Employee Benefit Plan. 1992.

LOS ANGELES TIMES MAGAZINE, August 23, 1987. *The Unsettled Self-Esteem of John Vasconcellos.* Los Angeles, CA.

LOS ANGELES TIMES MAGAZINE, June 14, 1987. *The Quest for Self-Esteem. Part IV.*

MEYER, R.G., AND HARDAWAY OSBORNE, Y.V. *Case Studies in Abnormal Behavior.* Boston: Allyn and Bacon. 1982.

MOGHADAM, H. *Attention Deficit Disorder: Hyperactivity Revisited.* Calgary, Alberta Detselig enterprises, Ltd. 1988.

MINDE, K., LEVIN, D., WEISS, G., LAVIGEUR, H., DOUGLAS, V AND SYKES, E. *The Hyperactive Child in Elementary School: A 5 Year, Controlled Follow-up Study of 91 Hyperactive School Children.* JOURNAL OF THE AMERICAN ACADEMY OF CHILD PSYCHIATRY. 11:595 - 610. 1971.

PARKER, H. *The Add: Hyperactivity Work Book for Parents, Teachers, and Kids.* 1988.

RAWSON, H. *The Englishton Park Program.* Hanover, Hanover College. 1993.

ROGERS, C.R. *A Theory of Therapy, Personality and Interpersonal Relationships as Developed in a Client-Centered Framework.* IN PSYCHOLOGY: A STUDY OF SCIENCE, ed. Koch. New York: McGraw-Hill. 1959.

ROGERS, C.R. *Client-Centered Therapy. Its Current Practice, Implications and Theory.* Boston: Houghton-Mifflin, 1951.

ROSENBERG, M. *Society and Adolescent Self-Image.* Princeton, New Jersey: Princeton University Press. 1965.

For Teachers, Parents and Kids:

ROSENBERG, M. *Conceiving the Self.* New York: Basic Books. 1979.

SCHULTZ, G.A. *The Relationship of Self-Esteem and Birth Order: A Study of Grade-Five Children.* Master's thesis. Edmonton, Alberta: University of Alberta. 1983.

SMITH, C. *Achievement Related Motives in Children.* New York: Russell Sage Foundation,1969.

SMITH, D.M. *Prediction of Self-Concept Among Learning Disabled Children.* JOURNAL OF LEARNING DISABILITIES, 12:664-669. 1979.

SNYGG, D., AND COMBS, A.W. *Individual Behaviour: A Perceptual Approach to Behaviour.* 1959.

STAINES, J.W. *The Self Picture as a Factor in the Classroom.* BRITISH JOURNAL OF EDUCATIONAL PSYCHOLOGY, 18:97-111. 1958.

THE JOINT COMMISSION ON MENTAL HEALTH OF CHILDREN. *Crisis in Child Mental Health: Challenge For The 1970's.* New York: Harper and Row.

TOLOR, A. AND DEIGNAN, M. *Adjustment Problems in Children.* SEATTLE: SPECIAL CHILD PUBLICATIONS. 1984.

WATTENBERG, W.M. AND CLIFFORD, C. *Relationship of Self-Concepts to Beginning Achievement in Reading.* CHILD DEVELOPMENT, 35: 461-467, 1964

WECHSLER, D. *Manual for the Wechsler Intelligence Scale for Children. Revised.* New York: The Psychological Corp. 1974.

WYLIE, R. *The Self-Concept.* Lincoln, Nebraska: University of Nebraska Press. 1961.

YANIW, L. *The Relationship Between Three Affective Variables and Student Achievement.* Unpublished Masters Thesis. Edmonton, Alberta: University of Alberta. 1983.

Subject Index

For Teachers, Parents and Kids:

Author Index

For Teachers, Parents and Kids: